D0734698

the faerie book

the faerie book

Samantha Gray

CICO BOOKS

London New York

Published in 2008 by CICO Books
An imprint of Ryland Peters & Small
20–21 Jockey's Fields   519 Broadway, 5th Floor
London   New York, NY
WC1R 4BW   10012

10 9 8 7 6 5 4 3 2 1

Text © Samantha Gray 2008
Design and illustrations © CICO Books 2008

The author's moral rights have been asserted. All rights
reserved. No part of this publication may be reproduced,
stored in a retrieval system, or transmitted in any form or by
any means, electronic, mechanical, photocopying, or
otherwise, without the prior permission of the publisher.

A CIP catalog record for this book is available from the
Library of Congress and the British Library.

US ISBN-13: 978 1 906094 92 8

UK ISBN-13: 978 1 906094 92 8

Printed in China

Editor: Marion Paull
Designer: Jerry Goldie
Illustrator: Emma Garner

Endpapers: "Faerie Land" by Emma Garner

Contents

PART ONE

What are Faeries?

Faeries live on an astral level as part of a spiritual world that is normally hidden from human eyes but coexists with our physical world. All faeries have powers of some kind, and can bestow good or ill luck on humans at will.

Iris, detail of the faerie, *John Atkinson Grimshaw, 1886, oil on canvas*

The World of Faerie

How and where do faeries live? What are their likes and dislikes? Can mere mortals visit? How can we tell if faeries are visiting us? The answers lie buried in tradition and faerie lore—and, with an open mind, can still be found today.

What's in a Name?

The name "faerie" is probably a combination of the words "fae" (friend) and "eire" (green). Faerie means literally "green friend." The Latin root is "fata," the name for the Fates, personified by three women who spin and weave the destiny of each person's life—"fatare" means to enchant. "Faerie" replaced the Old English "elf" during the Tudor period when Elizabeth I ruled England, and Edmund Spenser (c. 1552–99) and William Shakespeare (1564–1616) wrote of faeries in poetry and plays. Reflecting a rich variety of faerie lore, many different spellings of faerie are in use—fairy, fayerye, fairye, and fayre are just a few.

Faerie Temperament

The "once upon a time" and "they lived happily ever after" beginnings and endings of faerie tales are a human invention and not much to do with faeries. The world of Faerie is a place of dark enchantments, great beauty, and repulsive ugliness, mischief, humor, and joy, but also of envy and terror. Today we tend to think of faeries as being gentle, beautiful creatures and, of course, some of them are. However, our ancestors knew that they could also be tricky or even malevolent and possibly dangerous—and

Titania, *John Simmons, 1866, watercolor and gouache*

that they might take many forms. In the past, without all our modern technology, people were more in tune with the natural world and its spirits, and life included an awareness of faerie beings, good and bad. Mortals who met with them might be given wonderful luck or terrible misfortune. The wisdom of those times is full of warnings, terrifying stories, and advice on ways of appeasing faeries.

The Middle Kingdom

Faeries are sometimes portrayed as nature spirits, and at other times as supernatural beings or spirits of the dead. From Christianity comes the belief that they are fallen angels.

Faeries are usually believed to be of a middle nature between human beings and angels, inhabiting the twilight world of the Middle Kingdom. Faerie lore is rich in tales not only of faeries who have chosen to marry mortal men—a choice that rarely ends happily for man or faerie—but also of faeries who are

Faerie Luck

Faeries have the gift of foresight and can influence your luck for better or worse. Some stories tell of good luck bestowed in return for a good deed, but often these gifts seem to be handed out merely on a whim. For instance, in the many tales of human midwives called in to help with faerie births, some are rewarded with luck or money, others receive thanks, while the less fortunate only just escape with their lives.

punished by being condemned to a mortal life on Earth. In *Paradise Lost*, for instance, written in the seventeenth century, John Milton (1608–74) likens the fallen angels as they build Pandaemonium to "faerie elves." It was a popular belief that fallen angels, who had been ejected from Heaven and yet were not sufficiently evil for Hell, became faeries.

In Icelandic lore, faeries are descended from Adam and Eve after their expulsion from the Garden of Eden. As Eve washes her children, she is visited by God and, in fear, hides those children she has not yet washed. When God asks if all her children are revealed to Him, she lies and says that they are. God then replies that those children she has hidden will also remain out of the sight of human beings. These hidden children are the faeries and elves known as Huldre Folk in Scandinavian countries, and they deceive people as befits their origin.

A Vision of Loveliness

We now tend to use the word "faerie" to describe the tiny, winged females who have so captured our imaginations since the nineteenth century.

However, many other faerie creatures—some far less attractive, others even grotesque—inhabit the world of Faerie. They are invisible to most people, except for those adults who are attuned to the spirit world, some children, and animals. They are able to make themselves visible to humans at

*"Faeries, black, grey, green,
and white
You moonshine revellers,
and shades of night."*

The Merry Wives of Windsor,
William Shakespeare

will, though, and can be simultaneously seen by one person while remaining invisible to another.

Faeries do not have a set appearance as humans do, and are probably best thought of as consisting of natural energy. They may appear in physical form—sightings of them vary greatly

**A beautiful,
winged faerie**

in terms of description of size, and even color—or as a spot of pulsating light with a bright nucleus. Indeed, some faeries are particularly inclined toward "shape-shifting," transforming their looks entirely.

Faeries also differ greatly in character and temperament, and wicked faeries may be especially likely to shape shift, assuming the appearance of an innocent creature, such as an animal or even a baby, for their own dark purposes—but more on those sorts of faeries later (see page 94).

Are Faeries Always Small?

One common belief is that faeries are tiny, but as the Irish poet and faerie lore enthusiast W.B. Yeats (1865–1939) explains in *Irish Faerie and Folk Tales* (1893): "Do not think the faeries are always little. Everything is capricious about them, even their size. They seem to take what size or shape pleases them." Being of the material world, we humans are inclined to ascribe definite physical form even to spiritual beings. Yeats

"Transparent forms, too fine for mortal sight,
Their fluid bodies half dissolved in light."

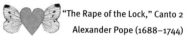
"The Rape of the Lock," Canto 2
Alexander Pope (1688–1744)

believed that faeries adopt any appearance that makes them more acceptable to a person caught unawares by the sight of them, proposing that they have: "no inherent form, but change according to their whim or the mind that sees them."

Faerie Garments

Since faeries have no set material form in the physical world, they do not suffer from being too hot or cold, and need wear no clothes at all—many choose not to.

However, since faeries are not so pure in spirit as angels, some do succumb to vanity, adorning themselves with pretty things, just as others—house faeries or elves—take pride in a well-kept house (and object to slovenly human owners!).

Nature faeries sometimes clothe themselves with leaves or petals, or in gossamer spangled with dew, and perhaps wear miniature hats, such as foxglove caps. Sightings of water faeries are usually of beautiful, slender, and naked females, covered only by their long hair.

Some faeries are known to cover up a part of themselves that reveals them to be something other than what they pretend. The Green Lady, or the Glasitig (see page 125), of Celtic faerie lore, for example, is reported to wear a long green dress that covers her lower half, which is that of a goat. In this way, she entices mortal men to fall in love with her.

Green, Red, and White

Some faeries may wear simple garments that identify them as belonging to a particular locality or tribe. Most people, asked about the color of faerie clothes, would answer "green" without hesitation, and they would not be far wrong. Green is

Fall faerie, *M. T. Ross, 1914, painted as an illustration to a children's book*

generally acknowledged to be the faerie color, particularly in Celtic countries. The Green Ladies of Scotland, for example, were—like many faeries—linked with the dead and so naturally wore green, which is the Celtic color of death. For this reason, green is so unlucky to mortals that many Scotswomen once refused to wear it at all.

Red is also a popular color with faeries, and in Ireland some of the tribes of small trooping fairies (see page 110) are said to wear green coats and red caps, while solitary fairies, such as leprechauns, the Cluricaun, and the Fear Dearg, prefer to wear mostly red. The poet William Allingham (1824–89) describes:

> "Wee folk, good folk, trooping
>   all together,
>   Green jacket, red cap, and
>   white owl's feather."

This seems to be the typical costume ascribed to the small trooping fairies.

The Lil' Fellas of the Isle of Man, about three feet in height, are described as wearing green coats and red caps, and are accompanied by hunting dogs of many colors, including green, blue, and red.

All sorts of domestic faeries seem to like wearing red caps. Green-clad faerie women enjoy a touch of red as much as

A faerie dressed all in green

the faerie men, and may wear tiny, exquisite red slippers. In Somerset in England, the faeries are said to wear red, and the rougher pixies green.

The Silkies of the north of England are believed to wear glistening white silk, the White Ladies of the Isle of Man white satin, and the Tylwyth Teg faeries of Wales white linen.

By contrast to this splendor, the house brownie (see page 78) is known to wear only ragged clothes—and is likely to take offense if humans present him with new ones. Pixies have no such qualms and the little pixie who is reported by Mrs Bray as making the following lament:

"Little pixie, fair and slim,
Not a rag to cover him"

accepted the gift of clothing laid out for him gleefully, chanting:

"Pixie fine, Pixie gay!
Pixie now will run away."

The Isle of Man is one of the few places where faeries are reported as wearing blue. In a guide to the Isle of Man, published in 1876, a farmer's wife is quoted as saying

"While every beam new transient colors flings, Colors that change whene'er they wave their wings."

"The Rape of the Lock," Canto 2
Alexander Pope

that her mother always maintained that she saw faeries, and described them as young girls with "scaly, fish-like hands and blue dresses."

Faerie Wings

Another common belief is that all faeries have wings. This is not so. Many creatures from the world of Faerie are wingless, but all have strong supernatural powers. A fascination for winged faeries developed

Faerie flying with butterflies, *unnamed artist in* Allers Familj Journal *(Sweden), June 24, 1925, page 3*

in the eighteenth and nineteenth centuries, when people also came to believe that faeries were tiny beings. Thimble-sized winged faeries are actually just one part of the Faerie population, but people's love of them is not surprising, given their beauty and—compared to some of the other occupants of Faerie—good nature.

Those individuals lucky enough to catch a fleeting glimpse of one or more of these tiny creatures have beheld wings of brilliant, constantly changing hues. Such myriad colors, pulsating

Faeries, Butterflies, and Moths

Winged faeries have always been associated with butterflies and moths. These flying insects are part of the family Lepidoptera, from the Greek lepidopteron, meaning "scaly-wing." Their wings are covered with many tiny scales that rub off easily, giving the appearance of an ethereal dust. Faerie dust, we can only imagine, must come from the wings of faeries and have magical properties.

Unlucky Opal

Faerie wings are often likened to opals because they reflect many colors. This gave rise to the superstition that opals are unlucky since faeries have supernatural powers that can bring people good or ill fortune.

with light, distinguish their wings from those of insects, and are a result of the powerful natural energies that flow through faeries.

Faeries, Insects, and Birds

In their various shapes, however, faerie wings are very much like insect wings. Some faeries have the narrow, elongated wings of a dragonfly, while others the compact wings of a bumblebee. Still others have large wings that are patterned like stained glass, similar to a butterfly's wings.

Unlike insects, faeries do not use their wings to fly. Instead, they sit astride the stems of plants, particularly ragwort, broomstick style, and fly using magic. They are also believed to ride on the backs of butterflies and birds, which are, we can only presume, their friends in the natural world. It may be that insects and birds are to faeries what horses and dogs are to people. Despite this, there are reports of long-standing enmity between faeries and robins, and nineteenth-century artists sometimes depicted scenes of faeries holding a robin captive. Robins are determined, strong-minded creatures, so perhaps this has led them to some kind of power dispute with the world of Faerie. We humans may never know for sure.

The Faeries have their Tiff with the Birds,
Arthur Rackham, 1906, ink and watercolor

Are Faeries Immortal?

This is another thing we cannot know for certain. The painter William Blake (1757–1827) reports having seen a procession of faeries carrying a faerie corpse on a rose leaf through his garden. The deceased faerie was buried with chanting and full ceremony before the procession vanished. Many suspect, however, that faeries do not have a mortal life and that their "burials" are charades in which faeries play-act the customs of humans.

Feasting and Sleeping

Do faeries eat and sleep as we do? It seems probable because faeries like to do what is enjoyable. Our ancestors warned one another never to touch faerie food for fear of becoming captive in Faerie, and many tales tell of mortals stumbling upon faerie feasts.

As for sleeping, what could be nicer than dozing on a warm summer's day? My mother always told me that spiders know when the day is to be sunny and spin their webs horizontally into hammocks for the tiny flower faeries. (In wet weather,

Magic Healing

"White witches"—healers in the time before modern medicine—frequently claimed that their skills and knowledge were a gift from faeries. During the famous witch trials in seventeenth-century England, Anne Jeffries, an Englishwoman investigated as a witch in 1646, said that faeries had given her healing powers.

they spin their webs vertically, so that the rain slides past them!)

Faerie Food

Sharing food is a faerie trait, especially for those faeries who live in close proximity to humans. Our ancestors used to leave out a dish of milk for them at night, and for centuries, gathering wild food from the fields for cooking, flavoring, and brewing was a natural way of life for many people. There was nearly always a jar of beer in the house, flavored with dandelion leaves, broom tops, or nettles—all flavors said to be much enjoyed by faerie folk. Herb beers are light, not very strong, and refreshing, perfect for quenching the thirst of humans and faeries alike.

May Day Recipes

The food we consumed in bygone times made it tempting for faeries to visit—or even to live in—the kitchen and help themselves to tasty morsels.

When my grandmother moved in to her ancient cottage in County Cork, she found a small collection of recipe books mysteriously left behind by the previous owner. Among them was a little book of "May Day Recipes" with a note on the flyleaf "for the good folk." The small book contained handwritten notes—such as, "Remember to plant the wild thyme near the hives for the bees"—on how to make some unusual delicacies:

Apple mousse
Blackberry jam
Candied angelica stems
Chestnut shortbread
Clover cake
Coltsfoot griddle cakes
Crab apple cake
Daisy leaf and cucumber salad

Elderberry turnovers
Frosted clover flowers
Gooseberry tart
Hawthorn jelly
Hawthorn leaf dumplings
Hazelnut cake
Nettle soup
Poppy seed cake

Rose petal sandwiches
Rowan jelly
Sorrel salad
Wild strawberry syllabub
Wild mushroom tart
Wild thyme scone

Beverages:
Broom beer
Coltsfoot wine
Damson wine
Dandelion beer
Hawthorn berry wine
Meadowsweet tea
Woodruff punch

Glamor

Faeries are able to cover themselves, and other creatures or objects, with an illusion that makes them appear to be other than they are. It is sometimes thought that the unearthly beauty of many faeries is due to this use of mesmerizing magic called "glamor."

Not only is glamor the means by which faeries can be seen by a person, if faeries so choose, but it allows them to appear in any form they wish. The more good-natured faeries usually appear in a form that will be acceptable to—and not frighten—people.

Cinderella

Probably the most famous instance of faerie glamor being put to good use occurs in the faerie tale *Cinderella*—the faerie in the tale is, of course, the faerie godmother (see also pages 76–8). When Cinderella cannot go to the ball, where Fate decrees she will meet a handsome prince, her faerie godmother uses glamor to change the appearance of things. Glamor transforms the dreary and mundane into the "glamorous."

Cinderella's faerie godmother changes a pumpkin into a magnificent coach, a rat into an impressive coachman, six lizards into footmen, and Cinderella's dingy clothes into "a magnificent dress of white silk, embroidered with butterflies and flowers of a delicate blue and sewn with seed-pearls." On Cinderella's tiny feet are the glass shoes that will play such a vital role in the denouement of the tale. Yet all is not what it appears to be and, once midnight strikes (a changeover time in the world of Faerie), all will revert to what it was, and Cinderella will once again be clothed in rags.

Faerie Struck

Using glamor, faeries can also make people appear to be other than they are. To be "faerie struck" is to be transformed in

Faerie Lovers in a Bird's Nest Watching a White Mouse, *Frederick Goodall, circa 1860*

shape to the beholder. In bygone times, when faeries wielded more power than they do in our modern age, tales were whispered of those who stumbled upon faeries uninvited being changed in this way—often into white mice.

Faerie Dust and Glamor

Today, faerie dust can be used as a metaphor for something precious that will turn the ordinary into the special, making life turn out all right after all. In this way, it is a physical embodiment of glamor.

In old faerie lore, from the time when people were less fascinated by harmless winged faeries and much more interested in the mischievous and even sinister ones who could imperil them, there is little mention of faerie dust. Some versions of the *Cinderella* tale describe the faerie godmother using magical dust to transform Cinderella, and Hans Christian Andersen describes the "Dream God," a storyteller who blows magical dust into the eyes of children to prevent them from seeing him.

In modern times, however, faeries are often depicted leaving a trail of dust as they fly, or sprinkling it from their wands. Although it has no historical basis in faerie lore, that is not to say faerie dust does not exist. In any case, the concept is beloved by children the world over.

Lost in Faerie Land

From our world, that of Faerie may be entered by secret paths and doorways, but only faeries know where they are and how to open them. Sometimes a traveler stumbles across an entrance by accident, and sometimes folk—often handsome young men, beautiful young women, or goodlooking children—are deliberately lured in.

Ancient lore abounds with tales of faeries stealing a human baby and leaving a changeling in its place (see page 94). And if you do chance upon the land of Faerie, tradition has it that you must not eat or drink anything because if you do, you may never be able to return.

Entrances to Faerie

The secret paths and doorways to the Faerie kingdom are reputed to lie mostly within ancient burial mounds or hill forts. Faeries, being from a spiritual world that coexists with our physical one, are often associated with the dead. This is why the Banshee (see pages 113–4), for example, is said to appear only when a member of one of the old Irish families is about to die and cross over to a spiritual plane.

Most faeries live in hidden places where nature has run wild. According to their element (see pages 36–51) they may live above or below ground, in or near water. Remote hills—rumored to be hollow and which can form a hiding place for gold— or secluded woodland, especially oak woods where bluebells grow, are likely faerie places. Some faeries prefer airy settings while other, less amenable faerie creatures, such as goblins, lurk in close darkness.

Under Water

The more treacherous of the water faeries live on the floor of the Earth's oceans. Their palaces are thought to be splendid, made of glowing coral, or of shells, polished pebbles, and glimmering glass-like stones.

Water faeries may also be found living in wondrous caves and beneath craggy cliffs. In freezing parts of the world, they live in ice cliffs from

which they carve walls, spires and battlements, caves and bridges.

The more benign water faeries live in or near fresh-water streams, rivers, ponds, and lakes. These faeries are said to be mostly smaller in stature

An elf peeps at a water faerie, *Leo Bates, illustration to* Where the Rainbow Ends *by C. Mills*

than salt-water faeries, and to make their homes within water plants and along banks.

Ancient Ruins

The crumbling remains of forts and castles attract some faeries, although even here they are said to make their homes beneath the earth, away from the gaze of mortals. When they hold their councils, revels, and dances, it is sometimes possible, if you put your ear close to the ground at night, to hear captivating faerie music rising up from under the earth. Once faeries are in residence, they lay down laws for trespassing mortals, who will be cursed by ill luck if they cut down a tree or carry away a stone. Most dangerous of all for mortals would be to attempt to build on faerie ground.

Hollow Hills

Some faeries, in particular Celtic faeries such as the Irish sidhe (pronounced shee—see also pages 106–7), live in palaces within pleasant green hills or

great rocks. Many of these "faerie hills" or "hollow hills" are still known all over Ireland, and tales of supernatural happenings surround each one. These faerie palaces are said to be very splendid. Lady Wilde describes them as "crystal caves, lit by the diamonds that stud the rocks."

Protection of the kingdom from trespassers is important, and those faeries who live in hollow hills warn away lost travelers or curious intruders with unearthly cries and stormy weather— powerful winds, sheet rain, rolling

Faerie living underground

thunder, and forked lightning. This is usually enough to deter most people but, if it does not, faeries send ill luck to blight their inquisitive lives. Tuberculosis, or consumption as it was once called, was linked to visiting faerie hills night after night, leaving the invalid hollow-eyed in the morning. At Castle Neroche in Somerset, England, faeries defended their hill from gold seekers by instilling the prospectors with dreadful panic—all the miners died within a month of the attempt. Mere mortals must remember to respect the hidden world of Faerie.

A sure sign that faeries are in residence is the bright emerald green appearance of the scenery, and the rounded, nearly conical form of the hills. No harm comes to unsuspecting passers-by, and cattle can graze safely on the nutritious grass. Faeries are believed to be grateful to the people who keep the hill pastures in good condition. If a farmer is careful of the roof of their dwelling and does not break it with tether-pin or spade, they show their thankfulness by driving horses and cattle to the sheltered side of the mound when the night is stormy. It was once a common belief that the faeries themselves swept the tops of the hollow hills every night, so that in the morning they were spotless.

Secret Island

The world of Faerie has long been thought to have its own secret island, which is known by many names, including Avalon, the Isles of the Blest (or the Fortunate Islands), Tir Nan Og (the Land of the Young), Tire Nam Beo (Land of the Living), Tirn Aill (the Other World), Mag Mor (the Great Plain), Mag Mell (the Pleasant Plain), Tir Tairngire (the Plain of Happiness), Tir-na-n'Og (the Perilous Realm), and Tirfo Thuinn (the Land Under the Waves). This last one refers to the belief that the island is submerged under water by day but rises to the surface at night. The island is marked on ancient maps, where it is shown divided in two by a wide river, and in the past, major expeditions were launched to find it but

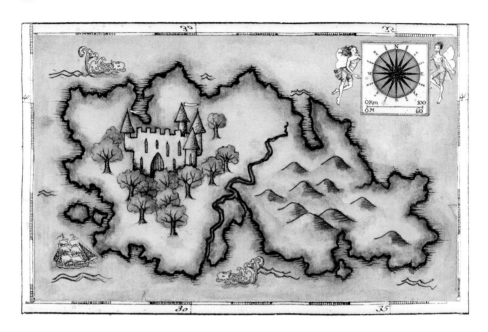

Map of the secret faerie island

whether they were successful or not we cannot know. Faeries do not take kindly to trespassers from the mortal world, and anyone who discovered the Faerie island is likely to have remained captive there.

Faerie Paths

In some areas, particularly where deep woodland, sparkling streams, and rivers are to be found, or where hills roll into the distance, interspersed by lush valleys, faeries have established their favorite pathways. They regard these as the equivalent of rights of way, which extend back through time, and houses built on faerie paths suffer from disturbance.

One such house in Ireland was filled with unsettling noises at night, and sounds like disgruntled whispering behind the walls. The owners slept badly and were plagued by all kinds of nightmares, waking to feel disturbed and unhappy. At the slightest breeze, the house would shake so that it seemed it would fall down. As no structural problem existed, the desperate owners finally contacted a clairvoyant. With her help, and that of a local historian, it was deemed that the corner of the house overlapped a faerie path. The corner of the house was trimmed off and, amazingly, peace returned to the house and the owners slept serenely at night.

In Ireland, believers in the world of Faerie would site the back door of their home opposite the front door. With both doors open, faeries were allowed free passage through the house, and so this was a mark of respect to the "good folk," whom they sought to please.

From Woodland to City

Our ancestors lived in a far less populated world than we do, where unowned land—often dark, impenetrable woodland—stretched as far as the eye could see, and farther. Along inhospitable coastland, dank and gloomy caves offered little respite. Moorland gave way to treacherous bogs and unexplored valleys. These were the places where faeries lived.

Travelers venturing into such wild and unknown lands were often led astray, even to their doom, by cunning faerie folk, but they were not the only victims of faerie enchantments and malevolence. Those people who lost their wits, suddenly languished in depression and unexplained illness, and likewise animals that sickened for unfathomable reasons were also thought to have

Favorite Faerie Paths

Faeries prefer to follow familiar routes, and these are likely to traverse special places:

Where wildflowers are plentiful
Crossroads * River banks
Woodland glades * Seashores
Old footpaths
Stairwells and halls in old houses
Coasts where estuaries meet the sea

offended the faeries in some way and been bewitched.

As the human population multiplied and took over unclaimed—by people, anyway—land, faeries, especially those of a vengeful nature, lost much of their power. Hostile to people, they retreated to any areas of wilderness left to them, while those of a friendlier disposition remained. They include benevolent faeries, and also the pranksters of the faerie world who enjoy playing harmless, if annoying, tricks on people.

City Life

Until the twentieth century, plenty of people had encounters with faeries and most had adapted to living with these whimsical beings. Some people, possessed of "the sight" (see page 156), were descended from generations of country-dwellers who kept the old beliefs intact; other faerie seers were visionaries, poets, and artists. They refused to be influenced by sceptics who, in William Blake's words, can only "see with, not thru, the eye."

"That, you must know, is the commonest way the faeries have of ending: they lock themselves up in a tower or within a hollow oak, and are never seen again."

Sleeping Beauty

Now, however, it seems that faeries have become wary of humans, believing them to be responsible for the destruction of their home—the natural world—and causing the displacement of woodland and flower faeries in particular. What has happened to these displaced faeries? One explanation is that they have retreated into hiding.

However, signs of faerie residence in towns and cities have recently been reported. Foremost in the news has been the Michigan town of Ann Arbor in the United States, where a new homeowner, Jonathan Wright, discovered a tiny doorway under his staircase. Since then at least twenty of these hidden doorways have been discovered in the town, the inhabitants of which have welcomed the idea of sharing their homes with faeries. There are no eyewitness reports of anyone erecting these miniature doors and, as Jonathan Wright admits, he could put them in "but that takes the fun out of finding them."

So it is possible that city dwellers are living in closer proximity to faeries than ever before, although not the really wicked ones that our ancestors had to contend with, which is something to be thankful for. We are quite likely, however, to find ourselves the target of faerie jokers—see page 87 to find out if you are already living with these mischievous creatures. The benevolent faeries bring us good fortune and guide us through life, so you will want to welcome such sprites into your home. You can discover how to create a home that will be visited—even lived in—by good faeries on pages 150–3.

A good faerie in the city

Faerie Music

Music from the world of Faerie is so enchanting that a mortal, once hearing it, is likely to remain forever lost in reverie. Those who become entranced by faerie music forfeit any hope of engaging with the mortal world—and worse fates may also lie in store for the afflicted.

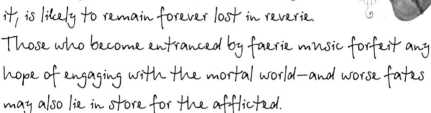

Some who overhear the haunting melodies become melancholic and spend the rest of their lives longing for something that feels forever just out of reach. Others, overhearing a vibrant faerie tune, are compelled to dance until they drop with exhaustion, or even die. From the oral traditions of faerie lore come tales of people who have danced until their toes have worn entirely away.

The Faerie Reel

Drawn to music—even to the music of the mortal world, and especially to the sounds of the fiddle and the violin—faeries sometimes haunt the lives of musicians. Folk musicians, in particular, have often described faerie encounters, and musicians of outstanding skill are in danger of being lured into the world of Faerie and held there. In Scottish faerie lore, for example, Thomas the Rhymer was spirited away to entertain the Faerie Queen for seven years.

The skill of the fiddler was often perceived to be not of this world, so much so that the crease on a fiddler's neck became known as "the devil's mark."

The Faerie Dance, *Robert Alexander Hillingford,*
oil on canvas

Sometimes fiddlers would overhear faerie
music and weave its rhythms with their
own. To be sure to show due respect to
the faeries, however, they would name
the tune something like "The Faerie Reel"
so that faeries would not become
vengeful toward them.

A musician touched by the genius of
faerie music may find that the intensity of
creative vision leaves him or her thin,
hollow-eyed, and exhausted, so that
genius suddenly flies away or death
comes too soon. As Lady Francesca
Wilde, writer and poet, who made a study
of Irish faerie legends, records:

"Wild and capricious as the faerie nature, these delicate harmonies with their mystic, mournful rhythm seem to touch the deepest chords of feeling."

Spell of the Faerie Harp

In her writing on Irish faerie lore, Lady Wilde relates a story about a victim of faerie enchantment of the kind once often heard about in Ireland. A gentleman entering a cabin in County Clare sees a young girl seated by the fire, chanting a melancholy song. On inquiry he is told that she once heard the faerie harp. Those who hear the faerie harp lose all memory of love and hate, and forget all things, and never more have any other sound in their ears save the soft music of that magic instrument. If such a spell is broken, the mortal will soon waste away and die.

Faerie Rings

Along with the love of music goes the joy of dancing. Faeries dance with wild abandonment, often in a kind of circular

Spirit of the Ceol-Sidhe

The poignant refrains of the Ceol-Sidhe (pronounced kayol-shee, the music of the Irish trooping faeries, see page 110) have made their mark on Irish folk music, which often expresses the sorrowful, yearning feelings of all those who have come into contact with the world of Faerie. Irish folk music is pervaded by gentle despondency, a sense that joy is just unattainable, and of foreboding at some unknown fate. Despite this, the sad, sweet notes of the melodies fill the mind and ease its restlessness. In faerie lore, the subtle charm of faerie music lulls mortals into forgetfulness of all things and sometimes even into the sleep of death.

reel. Faerie rings—circular marks where grass has been worn away—appear where the tripping and dancing feet of faeries have touched the ground, as described by the Irish poet W. B. Yeats:

"the faeries dance in a place apart, Shaking their milk-white feet in a ring ..."

Ancient faerie lore relates cases of mortals being drawn towards the evocative music, stepping into the faerie ring and being unable to resist joining in the dance. In faerie time, what seems like a single

Three faerie musicians fly through the air,
E. Gertrude Thomson, illustration to The Faeries *by William Allingham*

minute can last for seven hours, so that soon the victim of such enchantment collapses with exhaustion. Some are taken away to the world of Faerie, others are left in the mortal world—but for the rest of their lives, they seem distracted and "away with the faeries."

A Tale from Irish Faerie Lore

Many Irish tales describe how mortals have chanced upon faeries but this one, which is told in several forms, is one of the most fascinating. As is so often the way with faeries, its focus is music and dancing, beauty and enchantment.

On the eve between October and November, when the powers of the supernatural world are enhanced, the prettiest girl from the small village of Doneraile in County Cork ventured out for a walk. The day was soft and mild, and the girl wandered farther than she would usually go. Then, ahead of her, she heard the faint notes of some enticing music and she left her path to follow it. She soon came upon a crowd of faerie revelers and, afraid, she tried to run away but found she could not. The crowd parted and a handsome faerie prince held out his hand to her. Mesmerized by his bewitching eyes and good looks, she took his hand and he led her into the faerie ring and welcomed her into the dance. The moon and stars seemed to revolve around her head, and her feet did not hurt because she felt as if she was floating. All that existed for her was the sweetness of the music and the steadfast gaze of her faerie lover.

As the moon vanished from the sky, the music ceased. In front of the faerie crowd, the ground opened and a flight of silver steps led down to a splendid banqueting hall, which was glittering with the light from starry chandeliers that floated above their heads. The faerie prince offered her a beautiful golden goblet, and from the liquid it contained arose the fragrance of sweet nectar. The girl remembered her grandmother telling her never to drink faerie drink or eat faerie food or she would be lost to her family forever, and she paused.

At her hesitation the crowd of faeries became enraged and swarmed towards her. Panicking, the girl turned her back on the

faerie prince and ran up the silver steps that now seemed to spiral around and around so that she could not get above ground. She reached for the opening but it remained always just above her head, and she grasped and pulled at the grass and plants that she could feel beneath her hands. To her amazement, she found that she had picked a stem of athair luss (ground ivy), which her grandmother had told her is a powerful defence against faerie magic. With that plant in her hand she regained the open air, and she ran faster then she had ever done in her life to reach the safety of her home in the village—all the time hearing the clamor of angry faerie voices behind her.

At home, with her door barred, the girl went to bed but all night long she dreamed of the faerie music and, in her sleep, the faerie prince spoke to her in soft, sweet tones: "While you have the athair luss our power over you is gone, but I will wait till you dance again to our music in the faerie glen. Then I will hold you as my lover and my prisoner in faerie land and you will return home no more."

Being a sensible girl, she resolved never to go walking at the time of Hallowe'en again and to keep close to the village. She kept the stem of athair luss safely and the faeries never troubled her again. Yet it seemed a long time before her head was free of the sound of the faerie music to which she had danced that night in the glen with her faerie lover. Even when she was an old woman and had had a family of her own, at night she would sometimes dream that she was floating in the arms of the handsome faerie prince while the enchanted music played, and awake surprised to find herself old. In her bewitched dreams she was always young and could dance until the moon and stars left the sky.

Air, Earth, Fire, and Water

In the world of Faerie, as on Earth, nature has four vital elements—air, earth, fire, and water. Most faeries, depending on the natural feature with which they are linked, belong principally to a particular element. Those of the air are often called "sylphs," while "water sprites" live in harmony with streams, rivers, and other watery places.

When we think of faeries, we tend to imagine those whose element is the air, particularly the winged faeries beloved of novelists and artists. Yet different faerie beings are linked to the other elements. The Swiss alchemist Paracelsus, writing in the sixteenth century, described "the sylphs of air, the salamanders of fire, the undines or nymphs of water, and the gnomes of the earth."

Alexander Pope agrees with these faerie descriptions, adding: "The gnomes, or demons of the earth, delight in mischief; but the sylphs, whose habitation is in air, are the best conditioned creatures imaginable."

Devas, the "shining ones"

Nature faeries are thought to be part of the devic kingdom, an order that cares for all things natural, from the weather to plants and the landscape, water, and fire. Presiding over this faerie order are the devas, the "shining ones." Devas are closest to angels, being of high

Sylph faerie of the air, *Arthur Rackham, illustration to the 1908 edition of* A Midsummer Night's Dream

intelligence and able to protect and guide nature through their understanding of the divine plan.

Air Element

According to faerie lore, sylphs of the air can assume human form for short periods, and with their shape-shifting abilities, their size can vary from as large as a person to as small as a tiny insect. Sightings of them suggest they have wings.

Although people like to think of air faeries as kind and gentle, they can be temperamental and even volatile. Their natures are essentially as capricious as the wind. Wayward faeries have long been known to be behind strange, windy weather, and are known by a variety of names in different countries, from the Vejopatis of Lithuania to the Mbon of Burma.

They are, however, generally well disposed toward people. In fact, they are

believed to act as muses for those engaged in the creative arts, whispering words of inspiration into the ears of musicians, painters, and artists. Many sylphs are highly evolved, bringing together all four elements—their wings symbolize air, their legs earth, their radiance fire, and their fluid shape-shifting indicates water.

A faerie muse

These sylphs are not the only faerie beings of the air, though. Immense faerie creatures that resemble great dragons with huge heads, long bodies, and sinuous tails are rumored to live at high altitudes and embody powerful, natural energy.

Earth Element

Earth faeries are small, golden brown or dark green in color, and live in sociable, busy communities. They fulfill a valuable role in the devic kingdom, helping to energize the growth of plants and trees. Although they are impatient with humans, regarding them as something of a nuisance, earth faeries are completely benign. They love colorful stones and often collect them, storing them as a secret treasure trove.

Gnomes—Guardians and Smiths

Long before J.K. Rowling wrote about Gringotts in the Harry Potter series, gnomes had been identified as powerful beings from the world of Faerie, and were believed to be the protectors of secret

Never Betray a Gnome

Distrustful of people, gnomes are usually reluctant to have much to do with them. However, if a human does gain a gnome's trust, then he or she will have acquired a useful friend. Beware of betraying a gnome, though. Such an act is extremely risky because gnomes are relentless enemies and will certainly retaliate.

treasures hidden in caves beneath the ground. They were also the greatest of smiths. In faerie lore, Wayland is a famous smith renowned for producing exquisite faerie swords.

Although gnomes are of the earth element, they could more specifically be said to be rock faeries. These keepers of all the wealth within the Earth dislike humans taking it out. Most mining communities have legends of cantankerous gnomes—and their close relatives, the dwarves—cutting ropes and weakening shoring. It is said that gnomes and dwarves were once forced by mortals to work in mines underground. However, forcing them to work against their will was

An earth faerie

a dangerous business because they hold grudges till the end of time, and always take revenge.

Gnomes are said to dwell at the very centre of the Earth, and in many traditions it is claimed that they can walk or swim through solid earth with no more difficulty than we have walking upon it. In any case, being underground inhabitants of the world of Faerie, gnomes and dwarves must avoid the sun because even one ray turns them to rock, although apparently they do sometimes appear above ground in the daytime in the form of toads.

Celtic Mining Gnomes

The old Celtic communities in places that were once heavily mined, such as Cornwall and Wales, believed that mortal miners shared their underground workplace with supernatural beings— "the Knockers" were the gnomes of the Cornish tin mines while "the Coblynau" dwelt in Welsh mines.

The Cornish Knockers acquired their name from the knocking sounds that resonated on the walls of the mines just before cave-ins. To some miners, the Knockers were malevolent and the knocking was the sound of them hammering on walls and supports to cause their collapse. Others saw these faerie beings as mischievous but well meaning, and their knocking a way to warn miners and give them a chance to save their lives. To give thanks for these warnings, and to avoid future peril, miners cast the last bite of their pasties down into the mines for the Knockers.

For gnomes, the Coblynau of Wales were generous spirited, and actually helped miners by knocking in places with rich lodes of minerals or metal. Miners simply listened for the sound of tiny elfin picks.

Woodland Faeries

Although woodland faeries are mostly solitary, their habitat often brings them into close proximity with mortals. The Ancient Greeks called them "dryads" (see page 122), whilst in Malaysia they were known as the "bariaua"—shy and gentle supernatural beings. In Celtic lands they were the "green men" and "green women," and in England's West Country there is a saying that "faerie folks live in old oaks."

In Italian faerie lore they were the

"silvani" (wood men) and "silvane" (wood women), while the "folleti" were mischievous little woodland sprites. Woodland faeries are also found in German faerie lore, where they teach people how to make natural remedies. It was once customary to bake a small loaf of bread for these helpful woodland faeries, known as "wood wives," and leave it out for them in a suitable place. Rarely were woodland faeries seen to be dangerous, although the "saci" of Brazil could not be trusted and were known occasionally to harm mortals.

Some woodland faeries may be attached to a particular tree. They never stray far from it, and can step back into it if wary of some intruder. Other small

Knockers are Cornish mine spirits

woodland faeries make their home among the gnarled and twisted roots of old trees.

Fire Element

Salamanders—the faeries of the fire element—are the most powerful of all faeries in the devic kingdom. They inhabit underground volcanic regions and provide the energy for fires above ground and for lightning in stormy skies. Without these faeries, fire cannot exist. You cannot light a match without a salamander being present. If you ever need to light a campfire, call the salamanders and they will help you.

Like other nature faeries, salamanders are affected by the moods of any mortals with whom they come into contact. For this reason, anyone exhibiting fiery temper tantrums or stormy moods and thereby generating an inharmonious atmosphere at home or at work, runs the risk of inciting salamanders to create trouble.

A faerie tree, home of woodland faeries

The Basilisk

This fire-element creature has the body and head of a huge golden snake, but on its head sits a red comb like that of a rooster. It has two arms, which it uses to increase the speed of its slithering and to hold the front half of itself upright. It is highly poisonous and reputed to hate humans. The basilisk lives underground and it is, fortunately, rare for a mortal to come across one. Those who have are not likely to have lived to tell the tale.

There are many families of salamanders, differing in size and appearance. Some people see them as small balls of light, but most perceive them as lizard-like in shape and about a foot or more in length, although they can extend and diminish their size at will.

Hearth Faeries

An important household faerie belonging to the fire element was the faerie of the hearth. Paying homage to the hearth faerie for the gift of fire was customary in many countries. People neglected to do so at their peril and faerie lore relates many stories of revenge wreaked by offended hearth faeries. In Lithuania, the Aitvaras—the household fire faeries— were sometimes seen in the shape of flying dragons. In Russia, the Domovik lived behind the hearth and the family addressed him respectfully as "Himself" or "Grandfather." Mollifying him was advisable because he burnt down the house if offended. If the family moved, they welcomed their hearth faerie to the new home by using a brand from the old fire to light the new one.

In England hearth faeries, known as "drakes," were welcomed into the home, where they were perceived to be entirely benevolent. Not only did drakes bless the hearth, but they multiplied firewood and kept it dry—all in exchange for being given a home.

Water Element

The classical name for water sprites, or faeries, is undines. Beautiful and graceful as the water itself, they are sometimes seen riding the waves of the ocean. They can also be found in rocky pools, marshlands, rivers, lakes, waterfalls, and streams—any wild place with unpolluted water. They are covered in a shimmering substance that looks like water and shines with all the colors of the sea, but predominantly green.

Faerie lore suggests that undines closely resemble humans in appearance and size, except for those inhabiting

A water sprite

smaller streams and ponds. They make their homes in coral caves under the ocean, on the shores of lakes, or banks of rivers. Smaller pond undines live under lily pads and in tunnels of water weeds, and those who are in the charge of devas (see page 36) encourage the growth of underwater plants and compel the motion of water with their energy.

Gentle Women

Many water faeries appear as females of wondrous beauty and gentleness. In Spain, for example, the faeries of Cataluña, the Dones d'Aigua (maids of the water), are always kind to humans. They prefer to live in clean water, including wells, springs, fountains, and lakes, although they may also be found in nearby woods and caves. Half of their body can be fish or birdlike, and they often guard wonderful treasures.

The tiny Asrai, who reportedly live in Cheshire and Shropshire in England, rise

Rusalki, Polish water faeries

In Polish faerie lore, Rusalki are the faerie queens, and live in water for half of the year, where only witches dare to swim with them. When they leave the water they become sky faeries, mating with the thunder gods and causing thunder, lightning, and rainfall across the country in springtime. To thank the Rusalki for the rain that brings moisture to field and forest, people once placed wreaths of flowers on water during spring festivals, when they also danced in circles in celebration of these beneficial water faeries.

from the depths of their watery homes just once every hundred years and must return before sunrise, or they waste away. Faerie lore tells of a fisherman who caught one and, despite her cries, determined to bring her to land. By the time the fisherman made it to shore, the Asrai's cries had faded. All that was left of her was a pool of water and the fisherman had a welt on his hands where he had touched her to tie her up.

In Ireland, the Bean-Fionn wears a white gown and lives beneath lakes and streams. She is said by some to reach up to snatch children playing in or near the water, and drag them down, although this may well be an invention of anxious parents. In original faerie lore, the Bean-Fionn was known to be very protective of children, and a kiss from her was believed to render a child almost indestructible. She would, however, drown any adult she witnessed hurting a child.

She could be kindly to lost travelers, though, guiding them in the right direction. In England, she is called Jenny Greentooth or the Greentooth Woman.

Sea Faeries

All the seas around the globe have their population of faeries, sometimes known by the general term oceanids. They have been given a variety of other names by different cultures, but they share a common feature: they are usually women, approximately human-sized, of unearthly beauty, although with some kind of adaptation to their watery existence, such as webbed toes or even a fish tail (see Mermaids, pages 48–9).

Although male sea faeries are thought to exist, they are rumored to be peculiarly ugly. The Nucklelavee—male faeries

Sea nymphs, *Warwick Goble, 1920, illustration in* The Book of Faerie Poetry

who live in the seas around Scotland—for example, are half man, half horse in shape, with unattractive faces and ill tempers. They are extremely malevolent toward human beings. You can tell if one of these unappealing faeries is nearby because they emit a smell of rotten fish.

The Urisk is another Scottish faerie, who haunts pools. This solitary faerie is so lonely that he has been known to try to make friends with human beings, but his terrifying appearance usually scares them away.

Mermen, the male counterparts of the beautiful Irish merrows, are described as exceptionally repulsive. Covered in scales, they have pig-like features and long, pointed teeth. It is no wonder the merrows set their sights on mortal men.

Perhaps the general hideousness of male sea faeries is why the exquisite females have frequently been known to abduct young, handsome mortal men—in particular sailors, whom they are most likely to come across. The better-natured faeries help sailors to safety in storms, while wicked ones pull them under the waves even when the weather is calm.

Radiant Water Faeries

These are just some of the world's female water faeries who are renowned for their beauty:

Nixies (England): river faeries with translucent white skin, green teeth and pond-green hair; occasionally seen wearing green hats

Fenetten (Germany): lovely river women

Nereids (Greece): sweet and seductive

Loireag (Hebrides, Scotland): musical water faeries, who punish anyone who sings off-key

Bonga (India): beautiful maidens

Merrows (Ireland): sea faeries who long to seduce mortal men

Alvens (Holland): translucent faeries who can travel through air in a water bubble

Water wraiths (Scotland and Shetland Isles): ethereal water faeries who entice then drown sailors

Selkies (Scotland): shape-shifting sea faeries who often take the form of seals

Källräden (Sweden): enchanting maidens

Mermaids

Seafaring lore relates many sightings of mermaids, and descriptions of them are remarkably similar. A mermaid's upper body is that of a beautiful woman with long, rippling hair like seaweed, but from the waist down she has a large fish's tail with shiny scales.

Mermaids are most likely to be spotted in moonlight, sitting on a rock just off shore to comb their hair and admire their appearance in a shell-encrusted mirror. Like classic sirens, they draw men toward them with their eerily beautiful singing. Much feared because they seem to cause the drowning of handsome young men, seeing mermaids is thought to be a bad omen, foretelling storms and rough seas. As the onset of such weather creates opportunities for seizing the young men that they desire, it is likely that mermaids do appear in the mortal world at such times. Their victims are taken to a faerie land below the waves and their bodies never found; or else a piece of driftwood or some other object is transformed to resemble them and washed up on shore.

Mermaids sometimes bestow gifts, including magical powers, on mortals, but there is a high price to pay. In Cornish faerie lore—many tales of mermaids surround this south-western coast of England—a fisherman sometimes finds a stranded mermaid while beachcombing and helps her back to sea. For his efforts, the mermaid may grant him three wishes. For a time, say seven years, the fisherman uses the magical gifts conferred by the wishes for his own benefit, or that of his fellow man, depending on his character. At the end of this time, the mermaid returns to claim her ransom—the fisherman's life. Not only is he pulled

Mary Player

An English mermaid, called Mary Player, has only to circle a ship three times to sink it. A sailor's doggerel, adapted from an old German poem, tells her tale:

> . . . Three times she went 'round our
>   gallant ship,
> And around three times went she.
> And three times more she went 'round
>   our ship,
> And sank us to the bottom of the sea.

The Little Mermaid pines for her beloved, *postcard by an unnamed artist*

down into the deep but, every seven years, one of his descendants will be lost at sea.

The Little Mermaid

Perhaps the most famous mermaid is the Little Mermaid of Hans Christian Andersen's tale, the tragic story of a mermaid who falls in love with a prince. She gives up her voice to the Sea Witch in return for legs rather than a tail, and walks on the ground even though it is intensely painful to do so. If the prince does not fall in love with her, she has a terrible forfeit to pay. Choosing between her own life and that of the prince, she is transformed to foam. Feminists have objected to this tale, which supports a paternalistic society and encourages self-sacrifice in women. Luckily, the true mermaids of faerie lore would never dream of sacrificing their tongues and the power their singing voice gives them. The balance of power with mortal men is in the mermaids' favor.

City Under the Sea

In the seventeenth century, the crew of the *Lady Rosemary* reached land after traveling in remote seas, searching for treasure. Once ashore, they told a local villager of their distress at seeing one of their men drowned. The sailor had sworn he could see a beautiful woman, her head and shoulders bobbing among the waves, and her long hair drifting like seaweed. The crew all looked where he pointed, but no one else could see her. Entranced by his vision, and the sound of beautiful singing that filled his head, the sailor told his crew mates that he would swim out to the woman, rescue her, and bring her aboard, and so they lowered him down the side.

He was a strong swimmer and they saw him swim easily to a foamy part of the sea. Then suddenly it was as if unknown hands had gripped his ankles and dragged him down. It seemed he was in a kind of trance, so that he did not call back to the ship but vanished beneath the waves without protest.

"I will tell you what happened to your friend," said an old wise man from the village. "All who live around these parts know that there are beautiful women who live in the sea and their lower bodies are fish tails, though they hide these from the mortal men they desire. They make themselves visible at will and only to handsome young men. One of these supernatural sea creatures has dragged your friend down to the bottom of the ocean.

"Take comfort," said the old man, "the deeper he sank, the more his ears rang with a beautiful music that lifted his heart and filled him with a wild sense of joy. After passing through the levels of fish, the faerie women take mortals into clear water where they can breathe pure air.

"Reaching the floor of this watery world, he would see that it was paved with coral and shiny pebbles of myriad colors that glitter like sunbeams on glass. And before him he would see a fantastic city built of crystal and mother of pearl, and embossed with shells of many colors. And the faerie who took him will keep him with her and make much of him, as her own men are known to be uglier than any creatures here on Earth."

Mer-marriages

Water nymphs have been known to wed earthly lovers, and to live happily for a while, but sadness and separation are often the end result of such unions.

In this story from German faerie lore, a man who was lost in the woods came upon a castle, but found no one living there. For days and nights, he waited outside the castle until finally a young woman appeared. Thinking she must know someone inside, he asked her to find out if he may enter. She announced that she was the owner of the castle and that he may come inside. The two lived together, gradually falling in love, and he asked her to be his wife. She agreed under one condition—that he let her leave every Friday without asking questions or going to search for her.

They lived happily for many years until, one Friday, a stranger appeared at the door and asked for the lady of the castle. The husband, forgetting the ban, went in search of his wife, only to find her transformed, half fish and half human. She looked at him sadly and disappeared, never to be heard from again.

A water maid living in a castle

Faerie Festivals

Faerie enchantment is more potent than at other times on those days of the year when mortals and faeries celebrate the same ancient festivals. At these times, mortals who show due respect to the world of Faerie will be rewarded with good luck, or at least escape becoming "faerie struck."

An English custom for May Eve, for example, was for people to put trays of moss outside their doors at nightfall for the faeries to dance upon.

May Day

One of the cross-quarter days, which mark the midpoints between the solstices and the equinoxes, May Day on May 1 lies opposite Hallowe'en on October 31/ November 1 in the seasonal cycle. To the Irish Celts these two great festivals were Lá Baal Tinné (also known as Beltaine, Beltane, or Bealtaine), sacred to the Sun, and Lá Samnah, sacred to the Moon. The other cross-quarter days are Candlemas (Groundhog Day in the United States) on February 2 and Lughnassadh, or Lammas, on August 1.

The May Eve festival celebrates the birth of summer—a time when faeries ride out of their dwellings in the hollow hills and into the mortal world, and nature faeries rouse themselves from their winter rest. Green, the faerie color, is also the ritual color of the May Day festivities of mortals.

At this time of changeover, renowned for faerie mischief and enchantment, the

The Faerie Queen on her white horse

faeries are very powerful. The Faerie Queen rides through the country on her white faerie horse to entice away mortals to Faerie land. The Celts told their children not to sit in circles of yellow and white flowers at Beltaine because then they would surely be taken by the faeries. It is not safe to sleep out in the open air throughout the month of May, but especially on May Eve, because the faeries are looking for beauliful girls to become faerie brides, young mothers to nurse faerie babies, and handsome young men for the faerie women. Mortals hearing the bells of the Faerie Queen's horse are advised to look away and allow the faerie procession to pass by unseen—anyone stealing a glance at the Queen falls immediately under her spell and will be captured by the faeries.

Swimming and sailing are also dangerous activities on May Eve, because this is when the sea faeries arise from the depths for midnight revelry, and they will drown any mortal who dares to invade their privacy.

Talismanic Plants

Traditionally, Beltaine festivities began days before May Day. Villagers traveled into nearby woodland to search for branches and twigs from nine sacred trees, which were needed to build the Beltaine bonfires. At the same time, they gathered armfuls of rowan, fir, birch, and hawthorn to drape around the windows and doors of their homes the night before Beltaine, because these plants were known to ward off evil and to provide protection from faeries.

Before the fires were lit on Beltaine night, in the tradition of "May boughing," or "May birching," young men fastened garlands of greenery and flowers around the windows and doors of the girls they hoped would become their sweethearts. As with many such customs, the plant or tree from

Rowan tree

which the twigs and flowers were gathered carried symbolic meaning.

In the Isle of Man, crosses made of rowan were placed on front doors to repel faeries and mischievous spirits, while in Ireland kingcups were spread on stable floors to deter faeries from riding on livestock. Faerie rides caused all animals—except for cats (see pages 66 and 79)—to sicken and even to perish.

Another plant with magical properties useful for keeping faerie enchantments at bay, and for divination, was the marsh marigold, "the shrub of Beltaine." Garlands of it were hung over the doors of houses and stables to protect the family, as well as horses and cattle, from the faeries.

Magic of Hawthorn

Once called "bread and cheese" because the young leaves were added to sandwiches by country folk, the hawthorn was believed to be the most likely plant to be inhabited by faeries. Anyone sleeping beneath a hawthorn tree on May Day is liable to be kidnapped by faeries—

A faerie dancing on hawthorn branches

ground outside their homes, decorating them with wildflowers. The country custom of "going a-Maying" meant gathering these hawthorn branches, usually on May Day morning. The branches were interwoven before being strategically placed around the houses—the weaving was important because it strengthened the plant's magical powers, as did its covering of overnight dew.

Many communities elected a young girl as their "May Queen" to lead a procession, as well as dances and songs around the "May tree," or hawthorn, usually represented by a maypole decorated with ribbons, garlands, and a crown.

even sitting under a hawthorn tree at this time is risky because faeries dance on the branches and do not necessarily take kindly to human intrusion. It was once customary to tie ribbons or rags onto hawthorn trees at May Day as gifts to the faeries. For personal protection from faeries, many people carried a hawthorn twig tied together with twigs from an oak and an ash tree.

During May Day festivities, flowering branches of hawthorn were made into garlands, and people set branches in the

The Glastonbury Thorn

This celebrated hawthorn tree grows in St John's churchyard in Somerset, England. The original tree is said to have sprouted from the staff of Joseph of Arimathea, who had gone to Britain to spread Christianity. The tree flowers every Christmas and Easter, and each year its lucky blossom is used to decorate the Queen's Christmas breakfast table.

Tales of May Eve

In rural parts of Ireland, many tales are told of faeries seizing mortals on May Eve. The theme of each one is much the same, although the outcome may be different. In one, a goodlooking young man—the only, much-loved son of elderly parents—fell unconscious one May Eve while sleeping on a grassy bank. As soon as his parents and friends found his wax-like figure, they knew he had been taken by the faeries. They carried him home and laid him on his bed with much weeping.

The faerie doctor was called and gave the young man's parents a salve made of herbs to anoint his hands and brow every morning at sunrise, and every night when the moon rose. Salt was sprinkled on the threshold and round his bed, where he lay in a deep sleep. This was done for seven days and seven nights until the young man awoke.

"Why did you bring me back?" he asked. "I was in a beautiful palace where I danced with lovely faerie ladies to the sweetest music, and now it is all gone and I fear I shall never see that wonderful place again."

Then both mother and father wept and said, "Oh, son, stay with us, for we have no other child, and if the faeries take you from us we shall die of grief."

When he heard this, the young man felt ashamed and promised his parents he would never again on May Eve venture to the place where he was captured by the faeries. Still, his parents were relieved when he chose a mortal bride and the first signs of age appeared on his face, so that the faeries might not choose to seize him again.

In another tale, one May Eve a beautiful young girl lay down to rest on a mossy green hill at noon. She had a hard life, working in a dark windowless room, making shoes, and she was very tired and glad to be out in the fresh air. Soon she fell asleep on what was, unbeknown to her, a hollow hill. In any case, beautiful humans are in particular danger at this time of year when the power of faeries is at its height and they are watching for mortal brides and husbands.

The faeries were quick to spirit away the sleeping girl, leaving only a shadowy resemblance of her lying on the hill. Evening came on, and as the young girl had not returned, her parents and brothers and sisters went to look for her. At last she was found on the hill, lying motionless.

They carried her home and laid her on her bed, but she neither spoke nor moved, and by noon of the next day she was dead. As the story of her sad passing spread through the country, a faerie doctor came forward, who said he could bring the girl back from the land of Faerie.

A great crowd assembled to watch the faerie doctor performing his incantations by means of fire and a powder that he threw into the flames, causing a dense gray smoke to spiral up into the air. Then, holding a key in his hand, he called out three times in a loud voice, "Come forth, come forth, come forth!"

Amazed the crowd watched as the figure of the girl in a long white dress rose slowly up in the midst of the smoke, and she addressed her parents, saying, "Leave me in peace. I am so happy with my faerie lover, and my parents need not weep for me, for I shall bring them good luck, and guard them from evil evermore."

A young man, taken away by the faeries

March 15

December 25

April 30/May 1

November 11

May 4

November 8

May 11

October 31

June 24

September 29

August 7

Wheel of the Faerie Year

Encountering Faeries Through the Year

Mortals are more likely to encounter faeries on particular calendar days of the year. On festival days, faeries are more active than usual in the human world, and may create mischief. Other dates are significant in the faerie calendar because, for a brief time, the veil between the worlds is thought to become thin. Magic becomes possible as "doorways" separating the mortal world from the world of Faerie open.

March 15: Festival of the river nymphs and water faeries—a dangerous day for mortals to go swimming.

April 30/May 1: May Day (Beltaine). Faeries ride out from their hills on May Eve to celebrate the ancient festival.

May 4: Frustrating the Faeries. Irish day for confusing the faeries so that they will not create havoc for people.

May 11: Old Beltaine—blackthorn faeries guard the sacred thorn and will not allow it to be cut.

June 24: Midsummer Day

August 7: Faerie hills and dwellings are revealed on this day.

September 29: The door opens between human and faerie realms.

October 31: Hallowe'en

November 8: Again, the door opens between mortal and faerie realms.

November 11: Festival of the blackthorn faeries.

December 25: Christmas Day

Midsummer's Eve

The eve of the Summer Solstice, when twilight is the longest of the year, is a time for faerie revelry. This festival has been made famous by Shakespeare's *A Midsummer Night's Dream*. The Faerie King and Queen, named Oberon and Titania, with Puck (or Robin Goodfellow) and other attendant faeries, provide mortals with glimpses into the realm of Faerie. It is interesting that in Elizabethan England faeries were believed to be of the same size as humans.

Mortals once lit bonfires on Midsummer's Eve and mischievous or malevolent faeries would rush around the fires in a whirlwind to put them out. Just as on May Day, mortals could not enjoy fairs and festivals without thought for the faeries, but had to take steps to safeguard their family, livestock, and belongings from these troublesome beings.

Puck

Many stories surround Puck, or Robin Goodfellow, who is one of the most popular characters of English folklore.

In Shakespeare's tale, he is closely tied to the faerie court, but this is not usually the case—people living in rural areas might chance upon a puck at any time.

As a shape-shifter, a puck has many appearances. He often takes the form of an animal, particularly a horse, donkey, or eagle. The Irish Púca (see page 134)

The Reconciliation of Oberon and Titania, *Sir Joseph Noel Paton, 1847*

transforms himself into a horse, takes people on a wild ride and sometimes dumps them in water. The Welsh pwca leads travelers astray with a lantern that he blows out once he has taken them to the edge of a cliff. In the English midlands, being misled by a puck was known as being "pouk-ledden," and an old English expression for being lost was to say "Robin Goodfellow has been with you tonight."

On Midsummer's Eve, the healing, red-stalked Herb Robert is in bloom and mortals must take care how they treat it. Wantonly to destroy the flower, which is under the protection of Robin Goodfellow, is to court disaster.

Hallowe'en

The ancient Irish divided the year into summer and winter—Samrath and Gheimrath—the former beginning in May, the latter in November. Gheimrath was also called Sam-fuim—summer end—but these days, humans know it as Hallowe'en. At this time, when symbolically the Sun dies, the powers of darkness exercise great and evil influence over all living creatures.

On this one night of the year, the souls of the dead hold a festival with the faeries, dancing to faerie music till the Moon goes down. It is not wise for mortals to chance upon this revelry and, if they do, they may pay with their lives. In times past, it was the custom for food to be left out at Hallowe'en for the restless dead who had

Vila

These faerie beings from Slavic folklore were believed to be the spirits of the dead who could not rest in peace because they had not fulfilled their life's desires. At night they danced and, if a mortal joined them, he or she could not stop and would eventually fall down dead. The Vila, Willi, or Veela have power over storms, which they delight in sending down on lonely travelers. They usually appear to humans as beautiful women but can take the form of swans, horses, or wolves. Veela appear as dazzling witches in books in the Harry Potter series.

risen to dance with the faeries. If the food disappeared, it was a sign that the spirits had taken it, for no mortal would dare to touch or eat it. It was believed that a glance from one of the dead could kill, so on that night no one ever turned their head if they fancied they heard footsteps behind them.

The Dance of the Dead

In Celtic faerie lore, tales of fearful events befalling mortals at Hallowe'en are plentiful, and passed on in the oral tradition of story telling.

A man stayed out late one Hallowe'en fishing, and never thought of the faeries until he saw a great number of dancing lights. A merry crowd drew near him and, intrigued, he followed them till they came to the top of a mossy green hill. There they danced to beautiful music from faerie pipes and harps, and drank red wine from little cups. The man longed to dance with a lovely faerie girl, but she only said to him, "Take care, for the Faerie King is coming, and his wife, to see our fair."

As she spoke, the sound of a horn was heard, and a golden coach arrived drawn by four white horses, and out of it stepped a grand, grave gentleman and a beautiful lady with a silver veil over her face.

"Here is the King himself and the Queen," said the faerie maiden to the man, who was ready to die of fright when the Faerie King asked, "What brought this man here?" The King frowned and looked so enraged that the man nearly fell to the ground in terror.

Then they all laughed so loudly that the whole landscape seemed to shake with the laughter. The dancers converged upon him and tried to take his hands to make him dance with them, but he pulled away.

"Do you know who these people are, and the men and women who are dancing round you?" asked the Faerie King. "Look well, have you ever seen them before?"

And when the man looked, he saw a girl who had died the year before, and another friend who had died long ago; and then he saw that all the dancers, men, women, and children, were the dead in their long, white shrouds. He tried to escape from them, but could not, for they coiled around him, and danced and laughed, and, seizing his arms, tried to draw him into the dance, and their laugh seemed to pierce through his brain and stun him. He fell down before them and knew no more till he awoke next morning, lying within an old stone circle on the hill, his arms black with bruises where the hands of the dead had touched him.

The man went sadly home. He knew that the faeries and spirits had punished him because he had intruded on them on the one night of the year when the dead can leave their graves and dance on the hill in the moonlight, and mortals should stay at home and never dare to look on them.

The man in this story survived because he had resisted the Dance of the Dead so strongly, but not all were so lucky . . .

One Hallowe'en, a young woman coming home late grew tired and sat down to rest, when a young man approached her.

"Wait a bit," he said to her, "and you will see the most beautiful dancing beyond what you could ever imagine by the side of the hill."

She looked at him steadily and said, "You look like my sweetheart who was drowned, and as pale as the dead. Why are you here?"

"Look," he said, "at the side of the hill and you will see why I'm here."

The woman turned to see a crowd of faeries dancing to sweet music. Among them were all the dead people she could remember—every one of them was wearing white, and their faces were as pale as the moonlight.

"Now you must run for your life," warned the spirit of her sweetheart, "for if the faeries bring you into the dance, you will never be able to leave them any more."

While they were talking, the faeries had approached and danced round her in a circle, taking her hands in theirs and drawing her into the dance. Around and around she went until she fell to the ground in a faint, and knew no more.

She was not found till the morning, when the villagers brought her back hurriedly and laid her on her own bed at home. Her family saw that her face was as pale as one of the dead, and they sent for the doctor, who tried every measure to save her, but without avail. As the Moon rose that night, soft, low music was heard around the house, and when they looked at the girl, she was dead, and gone to the world of Faerie.

Girl surrounded by faeries performing the Dance of the Dead

Faeries, Witchcraft, and Familiars

In the witch trials of seventeenth-century England and Scotland, many of the accused cited the help of faeries in guiding them to perform their craft. They believed that this admission would stand in their defence, but such confessions served only to condemn them.

In common with witches, faeries were known to have supernatural powers. Witches and faeries were perceived as being part of the same world—perhaps for good reason, as you will read below—and both were seen as a real threat to mortals. Witches were burned on May Day during the time of the infamous witch trials, and for many years bonfires were lit on hills for protection and to drive away all supernatural beings, including faeries.

How Women Became Witches

During earthly festivals, when mortals are happy and carefree, the Faerie King and his chosen band of faerie men watch for the prettiest young mortal women to carry away to the world of Faerie. Faeries love youth and beauty, and the women are kept for seven years, until their looks begin to fade, when they are sent back to the mortal world. As compensation for this slight, the faeries teach the women secrets of their world, including spells and the mysteries of herbs, giving them magical powers to cure or ease diseases and ailments. In past times, "faerie doctors"—or witches—became very influential by these means. Their charms, spells, potions, and ointments could be used for evil or good, to kill or save their fellow mortals as they chose. They also had the ability to see into the future, prophesying at births and foretelling deaths.

Familiars

Witches are nearly always reported to live with a "familiar"—a subservient creature of some sort, usually in the form of an animal, that does their bidding yet exerts a peculiarly compelling force of its own. The witch appears to have control, but is also herself in the power of the

The Love Potion, *Evelyn De Morgan, 1903, oil on canvas*

familiar. Parallels between familiars and household faeries (see pages 78–82) abound, and many believe that familiars are actually shape-shifting faeries who

take on a recognizable form whenever they are seen by a mortal.

It has been observed that the nature of some witches improves under the influence of a familiar but that of others is actually corrupted. Such tales highlight not only the power of the familiar, but also hint at the variety of kindly, wise, mischievous, spiteful, and even wicked natures in the world of Faerie.

Black Cat

The witch's familiar was often a black cat, and it was once supposed that black cats have powers and faculties quite different from other felines. They were, for example, thought to be able to understand human speech and even to talk if they considered it judicious to join in the conversation. Their temperament was suspected as artful and deceptive, and people were cautious about caressing them because black cats might easily become cross and decide to cause injury or ill luck.

The Faerie Witch

In County Cork, in Ireland, a much-feared woman with magical powers used to live in a small but pretty cottage hidden in deep woodland. The woman was said to have been a beauty in her youth but she was now old, even though her eyes were still bright and sparkled like the stream that ran past her home. All around her cottage she tended herbs, in pots on window sills and walls, and in flower beds. It was said that she had a regular visitor—an owl from the woodland. Some claimed that they had seen her talking to the owl and that the owl seemed to understand and to nod its head, even to open its beak and appear to speak. Yet none dared approach to discover what conversation they had—if any at all.

People would travel many miles to visit the woman, who was variously called "the faerie witch," "the faerie woman," "the faerie doctor," and "the good witch," though no one was sure of her actual name. All the diseases and ailments that could not be cured by conventional means were brought to her because her knowledge of herbs was greatly respected, and people told tales of miraculous recoveries. Yet she never revealed the names of the herbs she used, but simply handed strange-tasting potions and unfamiliarly scented ointments to those people who sought her help. She gathered the leaves at twilight, or at dawn when the dew was fresh upon them. If the person who carried the herb medicine home let it fall to the ground, it lost its power; or if he or she talked of it or showed it to any one, all the virtue went out of it. It was to be used secretly and alone, then the cure would be effected without fail.

One time, a man from a neighboring town came to see the faerie witch for he was lame from a fall. The faerie witch knew he was coming because the faeries had taught her the power of divination, so she gathered herbs and brewed a potion, and it was ready for him when he arrived. He was very polite, as he had been forewarned he must be, and bowed before her and removed his shoes before entering her spotless home. He told her he had been walking in the hills and had slipped. The fall was slight but when he got up he found that his leg

was powerless, even though no bone had broken.

The faerie witch explained to him, "You trod heavily on earth beneath which faeries were resting, then annoyed them even more by falling with a thump on the top of their home. This made them so angry that they lamed you out of spite." She reassured him, though, that she was able to effect a cure.

She gave him the potion and told him to take it home carefully and use it in silence and alone, and in three days his leg would heal. Then the man offered her money but she refused. "I do not sell my knowledge," she said, "I give it so that the power I have remains with me."

The man did just what she said and, after three days, he was completely cured. He sent her a present—a hamper of fine foods—for he had been told by local people that a gift works no evil. If the faerie witch were to sell her knowledge for money, the faeries would take her powers away as surely as they had given them to her in the first place. Nobody wanted that to happen because they had discovered that to have a faerie witch living near them was really very useful.

Faerie Seduction

Many female faeries are bewitchingly beautiful yet prove deadly to mortal lovers. Even if they do remain in the earthly realm, these goodlooking young men are left sad shadows of their former selves. Likewise, compellingly handsome faerie men have stirred obsession in mortal women who have then pined away.

Over the centuries many tales have been related of handsome mortal men or beautiful mortal women whose families have been overjoyed to find them returned from the world of Faerie, only to discover them mad or sorrowful and wandering in their wits. In "La Belle Dame Sans Merci" (the Beautiful Lady Without Pity), John Keats (1795–1821) relates the story of a dashing knight who meets a beautiful faerie. Her beguiling looks speak of danger, but she convinces the knight that she loves him and he falls deeply under her spell as she sings "a faerie's song." However, she disappears, leaving him "alone and palely loitering." The poem tells of other mortal men, now ghost-like and ruined, who have suffered the same fate.

I met a lady in the meads,
Full beautiful—a faerie's child,
Her hair was long, her foot
*   was light,*
And her eyes were wild

"La Belle Dame Sans Merci," John Keats

La Belle Dame Sans Merci, *John William Waterhouse, 1893, oil on canvas*

Can Mortals Marry Faeries?

Mortal men, possessed by the idea of binding their faerie lovers to them, have been known to imprison them using iron, which faeries cannot pass, and beautiful mortal brides have sometimes been seized on their wedding day by faerie men who take the place of the groom.

It is rumored that these unions of mortals and faeries have sometimes produced children, whose descendants may have no special powers but may be particularly intuitive or charismatic. According to a seventeenth-century ballad, the original Robin Goodfellow, or Puck (see page 59), was the son of Oberon, the English king of the faeries and a "young wench." This half human, half faerie being became a trickster, who could shape shift so as to deceive mortals.

Most mortal–faerie marriages take place due to the capture of either mortal or faerie, but in some cases faerie women and mortal men choose to be with one another in the earthly realm. Lovely Welsh water faeries, called the Gwragedd Annwn, are especially renowned for occasionally taking mortal men as their husbands. However, there is always some stipulation to the union, and the faerie woman is likely to disappear back to the world of Faerie if, for example, her husband raises his voice to her or is in anyway disrespectful. As faerie ways can be difficult for mortals to comprehend, such marriages are mostly fated due to misunderstandings.

Time Travel

Mortals seduced and held captive in Faerie are often released once they have become older and less attractive, and they have no idea of how much time has elapsed in the earthly realm while they have been away. For example, a particularly goodlooking farmhand from Pembridge, England, walked out of the kitchen one night as his wife remarked that the broth for his supper was nearly ready. "Ay missus," he said, "I'll be back in a minute." He was captured by faerie women and lost for 23 years, but his time in the world of Faerie seemed so brief that when he walked back in to his home, he asked, "Well, missus, is my broth ready?"

A faerie enchantress tempts a young
mortal man

However, although for a mortal and
faerie to fall in love is usually doomed, it
is believed that the secret faerie island
(see pages 25–6) offers a safe haven for
such couples, who can live happily there.

Faerie Enchantresses

Beautiful, dangerous faerie women have
been given different names around the
world. On the Isle of Man there is the
Lhiannan Shee, who, in Ireland, is called
the Leanan Sidhe (lan-awn-shee), or
"Faerie Mistress." Once she has a
handsome man in her embrace, she
draws out his spirit gradually, continuing
to visit him over time, but leaving him
ruined. He will waste away and even go
mad, but he is also likely to become
intensely emotional and brilliantly
creative. As W. B. Yeats writes:

"She is the Gaelic muse, for she gives inspiration to those she persecutes. The Gaelic poets die young, for she is restless and will not let them remain long on earth—this malignant phantom."

The only way a victim can escape the Faerie Mistress is to find another to take his place.

Scandinavia's Skogsrå live in forests, over which they rule like queens. Rumors about these faerie enchantresses are

The Snow Queen

In this story by Hans Christian Andersen, the Snow Queen is a faerie enchantress of the north pole, described as dazzling in her loveliness and as beautiful as the ice crystals themselves. She enchants Kay, a mortal boy, who is the victim of a troll-made magic mirror, which distorts his eyes and heart so that he is cruel to those he once loved. The Snow Queen carries Kay away with her, kissing him once to warm him from the cold and a second time to wipe his memory clean of any other loves; but she forbears to kiss him three times because this would kill him. Even so, Kay is believed dead in the mortal world where he is said to have drowned in a river.

Kay and the ice-blocks, *Cecile Walton, illustrating Andersen's faerie tale*

many. Some believe they desire handsome mortals but their touch is fatal; others say that they enhance the lives of men who have granted them sexual favors so that such men's lives are marked by extraordinary good fortune. In India, the Bonga Maidens are water faeries who entice mortal men to fall in love with them, and may even marry one. To Native American tribes, faerie enchantresses were beautiful, supernatural Deer Maidens who lured men to their doom.

To Iranians, faeries are Feroüers, or Peris, and many tales surround Dukhtari Shah Periân (Daughter of the King of the Faeries). She is so beautiful that even the thought of her is enough to make men long for her in vain for, if they behold her, they must die.

In the depths of eastern Europe, a beautiful young faerie in a white dress, known as the phantom of the Ukraine, meets lonely wanderers in the snow. With her kisses she lulls men into a fatal sleep from which they never awake.

An artist's stare

These days, mortals descended from faeries—often entirely unbeknown to them—have the potential to invest those upon whom they gaze with an obsessive infatuation that feels like love. Since those with faerie ancestry are drawn to creativity, it is often musicians, artists, and poets who can make themselves adored by any person they look upon, simply by the power of their glance.

Faerie Seducers

Male faeries can look into a mortal woman's eyes and make her believe that she is more special than any other who has ever lived. Under this spell, a mortal woman can feel intensely alive and so happy that she cannot imagine ever feeling such joy again. Her faerie lover can read her very thoughts so that she feels only he has ever really known her. This is how male faeries bewitch mortal women. Later, a victim of faerie seduction can pine away with longing.

Spellbound

To look into the eyes of a faerie is to become spellbound. One intense stare leaves mortals in a death-like trance. Their real bodies are carried off to the world of Faerie and a clothed shadow of human form is left in their place.

There were once faerie doctors who specialized in relieving faerie-induced ills, such as those resulting from the faerie glance. Through incantations it was sometimes possible to persuade faeries to return their mortal prize.

An ancient spell for compelling a person to fall in love, together with the faerie glance, works a powerful magic. In the eighteenth century, a young man living in County Limerick, in Ireland, possessed an unusual power over women. He was witty and had the soulful eyes that indicate passionate, poetic natures.

One day he was traveling far from home and, feeling hungry and weary from his journey, he stopped at a grand house to request a drink of milk. The daughter of the house, shy and not liking to admit a stranger when she was alone, refused him entry.

The young poet fixed his eyes earnestly on her face for some time in silence, then left and walked slowly toward a small grove of trees just opposite the house. There he stood for a few moments resting against a tree, and facing the house, as if to take one last glance, vengeful

A man with a touch of faerie writes a love spell

or admiring. Then he went on his way without once turning round.

Watching him from a window, the girl felt compelled to go after him and she followed like one in a dream, step by step, down the road. She passed her father, whom she appeared not to see. Even when he shouted loudly for her to stop, she never paid heed. Spying a rolled piece of paper tied to a branch of the tree where the poet had rested, the father took it down out of curiosity. The moment he untied the knot of string that bound the paper roll, he saw his daughter, in the distance, suddenly stop walking and flop to the ground like a rag doll. He ran to her and helped her up, then led her back to the house.

Once safe inside her home, the girl explained that she felt herself drawn by an invisible force to follow the young stranger wherever he might lead. She said she would have followed him through the world, for her life seemed to be bound up in his; she had no will to resist, and was conscious of nothing else but his presence. Suddenly, however, the spell was broken, then she heard her father's voice, and knew how strangely she had acted. At the same time the power of the young man over her vanished, and the impulse to follow him was no longer in her heart.

The paper, on being opened, was found to contain five mysterious words written in blood, and in this order:

$$S A T O R$$
$$A R E P O$$
$$T E N E T$$
$$O P E R A$$
$$R O T A S$$

These letters are so arranged that read in any way—right to left, left to right, up or down, the same words are produced. When written in blood by a person with a touch of the faerie about them, and with a pen made of an eagle's feather, they form a love charm that no mere mortal can resist.

Well-behaved Faeries?

These days, we love to believe in good faeries, but our ancestors knew better. Even well-intentioned faeries can be capricious and take offense if mortals do not comply with their own bizarre set of standards. Faeries, after all, inhabit the Middle Kingdom, and are not angelic enough for Heaven.

Faerie Godmothers

Our favorite faerie tales, such as *Cinderella* and *Sleeping Beauty*, have faerie godmothers who come to the rescue of good mortals and help to transform their lives with magic—or glamor (see page 20). We have come to believe that faeries might be like guardian angels or spirit guides—they are not. They are much too preoccupied with their own interests to watch over mortals with kindly concern. Faeries are, of course, perfectly capable of effecting magic, just as the faerie godmothers do in these much-loved tales . . . but in the service of mortals rather than themselves? Do faeries help to win handsome mortal princes for beautiful mortal princesses? Such altruism is not in the faerie nature. They are far more likely to carry off goodlooking youthful mortals for themselves and hold them captive in the world of Faerie.

In the old faerie lore, sources for *Cinderella* and *Sleeping Beauty*, faerie godmothers are not present. For example, in the Grimm Brothers' *Cinderella* of 1812, the put-upon heroine is helped by the spirit of her dead mother. Two white pigeons assist Cinderella with her chores and tell her to visit her mother's grave where she finds a beautiful ballgown awaiting her. Faerie godmothers were added to *Sleeping Beauty* by Charles Perrault in the seventeenth century; no such figures appear in his source, *Sole, Luna e Talia* by Giambattista Basile.

Faerie godmothers are linked to the three Fates of Greek mythology, who bestowed gifts—good and ill—on newborn babies. The Fates were not always benevolent and could be cruel as well as kind. This is reflected by the different faerie godmothers in *Sleeping Beauty*. One of them, a wicked old faerie who, offended at not being invited to the

Sleeping Beauty in the Woods and her faerie godmothers, *F. Thiriet, Perrault's Tales*

christening, decides to bestow a curse on the innocent mortal baby. Our perception of faerie godmothers is one in which our

A faerie godmother

ideas about guardian mother spirits, or angels, and faeries overlap. Faeries can certainly transform mortal lives with glamor and hold us spellbound but, unlike guardian angels, they do so for their own purposes.

The Brownie

A small, dwarf-like male household faerie, the brownie seems to prefer homes in the wild rural areas of northern England and Scotland, but humans in many other places have also suspected the presence of a brownie. This apparently humble and unobtrusive being from the world of Faerie serves mortals in a manner true to his own obsessive nature. Cleaning, cooking, carrying out farmhouse errands, such as ploughing, grinding grain, and churning butter, the brownie makes himself indispensable.

Wearing tattered, brown clothes, and a brown, hooded cape, or naked and covered with long, shaggy hair, the brownie has eyes as black as coal, slightly pointed ears, and long, nimble fingers. He is active only at night, usually finishing the housework that has been left undone by mortals. Rarely seen, the brownie can often be heard cleaning, scrubbing, and creeping about the house, looking for dirt and dust. He becomes extremely devoted to a house or family, or both. Frequently, a brownie will adore a certain individual from a family and set him or her on a pedestal—this person can then do no wrong in the brownie's eyes and gets special treatment. A brownie who has become attached to a particular individual or family—as brownies often do with old families—will follow that person or family wherever they move to, even to a different continent.

Retribution and Reward

Unsurprisingly, mortals whose homes have a brownie are often keen to keep their resident night-time cleaner and take steps to ensure his happiness. This is

Ask your Cat

Earth-element, household faeries often resemble goblins in appearance. The best way to find out if you have one is to ask your cat, if you have one of those. Faeries welcome cats into their world and it is said that if a faerie, such as a brownie, is present in the home, the cat would know and tell its owner. It is, of course, the responsibility of the owner to understand the cat's form of communication. This is why it is helpful to ask your cat directly. If the answer is "yes," the cat will give a simple nod and blink its eyes once.

wise because a neglected brownie, or one disgusted by the slovenliness of humans, can turn bad and become very troublesome indeed. The first signs of a disgruntled brownie include furniture pushed out of place and items of great necessity to their owner being hidden. Pairs of glasses, for example, are apt to be slid out of sight, as are keys; and single socks will be removed from baskets of clean washing. Many of those who believe they have a brownie in their home report how these faeries have adapted to the modern world, punishing mortals for perceived offenses by hiding their cell phones and TV remote controls. This is likely true, for brownies are observant creatures and quick to spot the habits of humans.

In return for his hard work, a brownie will accept gifts of food—fresh milk or cream, honey, bread, or beer may be put out for him—but only if they are put where he might come upon them "accidentally." Other gifts offend him. The mistake most often made by mortals who are keen to look after their brownie, and horrified by the sorry state of his apparel, is to leave out a new set of clothes for him. Nothing offends a brownie more than this. He might put on his new clothes but he will certainly leave the home forever, despite his previous obsessive devotion. His last words as he exits are said to be:

> "What have we here, Hempen, Hampen!
> Here will I never more tread nor stampen."

Dobby, the House Elf

Now famous thanks to J.K. Rowling's Harry Potter series, the dobby is a house elf which has long been known to be an exceptionally gentle and well-meaning relative of the brownie. Like the brownie, the dobby—also known as Master or Mister Dobbs—emerges at night to complete any unfinished chores. In Sussex, England, "Master Dobbs," as a dobby is called there, is especially kind toward elderly mortals, who are likely to welcome his support and assistance around the home.

Dobbies resemble brownies except that they are thinner and some have no noses, only nostrils. In certain regions, dobbies even have webbed fingers that are joined completely except for the thumb.

Hob Headless

Not all hobs are benevolent. There is one tale of a sinister hob, Hob Headless, who haunted a road in north Yorkshire, England, but luckily couldn't cross a river that flowed into the trees, and so was contained in a particular place. His many activities included pouncing on unsuspecting travelers to frighten them, changing the direction of signposts, and causing vehicles to skid on the road. He was eventually exorcised and banished to a hole beneath a large stone by the roadside for 99 years and a day. The stone itself is cursed, and it is believed that anyone who sits on it will never be able to get up—a curse the power of which has gone untested, not surprisingly. The 99 years is now nearly up, so there may soon be more tales of trouble from north Yorkshire concerning Hob Headless.

Hob, Specialist Worker

Also called a hobbe, hobby, hobredy or hobany, hobs resemble brownies in appearance. However, they specialize in particular types of work, as opposed to their jack-of-all-trades cousins, and they can be mischievous if bored. They tend to attach themselves to families in need. One of them, known as Hobhole Hob, who lived not in a mortal home but in his own cave, was renowned for curing whooping cough. Parents would bring their sick children into his cave and whisper,

> "Hobhole Hob! Hobhole Hob!
> Ma bairns gotten t'kink cough,
> Tak't off; tak't off"

and the child would be cured.

In other parts of the world, hobs are known by different names. In Cologne, Germany, for example, Heinzelmann, or Heinzelmmanchen, are friendly household faeries who work in shops—often bakeries—during the night, with such great skill that the shopkeepers require fewer assistants. It is impossible to describe their appearance because they have never been seen, but their work

A housekeeping faerie

is beyond dispute and their superb craftsmanship always appreciated.

"Our Housekeeper"

The Bean-Tighe (ban-tee or ban-teeg), meaning "woman of the house," is a kind and gentle Irish housekeeping faerie, sometimes simply referred to as "our housekeeper." These faeries appear as tiny elderly women with dimpled faces, and are dressed in the old-style garments of peasants. Adopting a mortal home to live in, they love to help mothers tend to children, pets, and household chores. If you live in a rural setting in a home with children and a fireplace, you may be able to get a Bean-Tighe to take up residence at your hearthside. Call for one with an offering of her favorite food—strawberries and cream. If she comes to your home, she will bless it and all who live there, even if she decides not to stay.

The Tooth Faerie

In some European faerie lore, brownies, or house elves, will perform useful tasks or exchange valuable treasures for things mortals view as mundane or useless. The tooth faerie, who replaces a baby tooth hidden under a child's pillow with a coin, has now been adopted as an idea by parents keen to ease the way for a child to part with something of his or herself. Yet faeries truly are known to value teeth—just like the Vikings, who gave a "tooth fee" for valuable baby teeth. In the past, these treasured tokens were believed to ward off witches and demons.

Boggarts—Troublesome Faeries

While brownies are helpful to have around the house, boggarts are quite the reverse. The boggart is believed by some to be a cousin of the brownie and by others to be a brownie turned bad, usually as a result of some mortal insult—real or imagined. Just like brownies, boggarts are invisible except if they choose not to be. This troublesome earth-element faerie is dirty and unkempt-looking, and nearly always wears a cross expression. The only time he doesn't is when he is taking spiteful pleasure in playing some ghastly prank on another member of the household. If your home is plagued with more than its fair share of mishaps, it just may be that a boggart has taken up residence.

Things that go Bump in the Night

Typical signs that you are unfortunate enough to be sharing your home with a boggart include finding yourself unusually clumsy, or noticing that the household seems to get messy of its own accord. For example, if you are sure you put a cup or glass down carefully on a table yet it tips over the side, spilling the contents everywhere, you are probably living with a boggart. Do you find that electric cables wind around one another to create an untidy tangle? Boggarts love to do this. A dropped piece of toast will always land buttered-side down if you are living with a boggart, who scampers invisibly across the room to flick it around in mid-air. Boggarts jump up and down on squeaky floorboards while you are trying to sleep, open and close creaking doors, and make odd rattling sounds. Sometimes, just for the heck of it, they will push a plate off a kitchen surface, or an ornament off the mantlepiece, because they enjoy seeing much-loved china shatter into pieces.

Permanent Residents

The bad news is that, no matter what you do, it is likely that your boggart is with you to stay. No amount of feeling unpopular will worry the boggart, who thrives on an atmosphere of frustration and annoyance. People have tried exorcising the boggart, which sometimes works. Others recommend giving the boggart a taste of

his own medicine by becoming as annoying as he is—singing loudly off tune, or whistling, for example, as well as hanging bells on the doors, and clattering pots and pans while you cook. The problem with this method is that you are upping the stakes for the boggart, who may redouble his efforts—and if you share your home with other people, they are likely to object.

Traditionally, boggarts particularly favor the English counties of Lancashire and Yorkshire, as reflected in several place names in the area—Boggart's Clough and Boggart's Hole, for example. But when people, driven demented by a boggart, have actually tried moving home, it is only to find that their boggart has accompanied them, no matter where they go.

A boggart causing mischief

Discourage entry

To guard against a boggart entering the home, put iron nails on window sills and hang iron horse shoes above doors. Such tactics will not chase out a boggart already in residence, but it may prevent one from coming into your home in the first place.

Mischievous Faerie Tricks

Earth faeries, such as the boggart, are not the only ones who cause trouble to mortals. Faeries of the air element delight in playing harmless tricks on humans—just because they can.

Noisy tricks

Not even cats—usually given special privileges by faeries—escape the horrid attentions of the boggart, who will pull their tails and whiskers and make them howl. Dogs detest boggarts, who torment them so that the dogs bark incessantly. Boggarts even prod sleeping babies to make them cry. The joy of such misdeeds for the boggart is that humans, in turn, are tormented by the noise.

Faeries of the air do not engage in really bad behavior, in the way that cross or wicked faeries do—they would never pinch mortals or trip them up. However, they do delight in the irrational. This is why there is always a piece of cutlery—often a spoon—left in the bottom of the washing-up bowl once you've poured the water away.

Queen Mab

Mab, the Faerie Queen of the Night, is often portrayed as a trickster. She expected all to be in order before the household retired to bed. However, if this were not so, the offenders would be pinched by faeries:

> Wash your pails, and cleanse
> your dairies;
> Sluts are loathsome to the faeries:
> Sweep your house; who doth not so,
> Mab will pinch her by the toe.

Robert Herrick

It is known that mischievous fairies are nearly always thought to have been responsible for the small annoyances of life. Tangles in human hair, for example, and horses' manes are traditionally known as "elf-locks," so Queen Mab "plats the manes of horses in the night; and bakes the elf-locks in foul sluttish hairs, which once untangled much misfortune bodes"—as well as all sorts of other acts of mischief—as Mercutio tells us in William Shakespeare's *Romeo and Juliet* (Act 1, Scene 4).

Queen Mab, *Henry Fuseli, 1814, oil on canvas*

Faerie Gold

Unsurprisingly in the unpredictable world of Faerie, two entirely contrary beliefs surround the concept of faerie gold. One recurring theme is that a faerie gift that seems worthless, such as dead leaves or wood shavings, turns into gold. The other, a belief of the Celtic lands, is quite the opposite—faerie gold looks valuable but is really worthless, something invested with glamor (see page 20). Faeries are wounded by the touch of gold, supporting the Celtic idea that they use only faerie gold in their traffic with mortals, which turns to detritus from the woodland floor at the first sunset after its creation.

Slut's Wool

The grey fluff, traditionally called slut's wool, which lurks behind doors, in corners, and under furniture is a favorite item for naughty faeries. They might twist it to your hair as they tie it into knots while you sleep. Sticking the wool, or strands of your hair, onto soap is another trick. Of course, if they get the chance, they will drop a speck onto camera lenses, too.

Faerie Fun

Along with their enjoyment of traditional pranks, faeries have discovered new ones for the modern world. These are just a few of the ways that faeries might be having fun at the expense of mortals:

☆ Flicking contact lenses off the ends of people's fingers.

☆ Giving pens and pencils a shove so that they roll off the edges of desks.

☆ Stealing pens, or their caps, and kicking any pen in your pocket to make its ink run.

☆ Hiding a small piece of self-assembly furniture then sliding it back into view just as you think you've finished.

☆ Jumping around on your computer keyboard so that the program you are running inexplicably crashes.

☆ Helping themselves to delicious food, such as scrumptious cake, by pilfering tiny pieces under the noses of those eating it.

☆ Pulling loose threads on jumpers or the hems of garments and snagging pantyhose.

☆ Dropping stains onto freshly laundered clothes.

☆ Pulling buttons loose and untying shoelaces.

☆ Dancing on top of electric light bulbs with damp feet until the lights flicker and go out.

☆ Blowing out matches as you try to light candles.

☆ Dropping sharp little items into shoes to give you a nasty surprise when you slip your feet in.

☆ Keeping you awake at night by tickling you as you are about to doze off, or jumping on an arm or a leg so that you twitch awake.

☆ Tickling dogs to make them scratch—a scratching dog may have a case of faeries, rather than fleas. Faeries will also tickle the ends of dogs' noses to make them sneeze—they would never do this to cats.

The Shadowy Side of Faerie

Malevolent faeries mete out sickness, ill luck, or even death just when the idea comes to them. Mortals who do no wrong may still become the victims of sinister spirits from the dark side of Faerie land, while interrupting faerie revelry (see pages 52–57) is an offense punishable by death or madness.

In days of old, when we were closer to the natural order of things and faeries had more power, evil faeries were very much feared for the terrible harms they could inflict. The only way to avoid the havoc they could wreak was to be respectful to all faeries and find ways to placate them.

Wicked Ways

Particular ailments or injuries suffered by mortals are renowned for being caused by faeries. Inexplicable bruises, for example, were due to being pinched by malicious pixies. What today we call a "stroke" was once called "elf stroke," or "the touch," and was believed to be the result of evil faeries stroking their victims into seizures. We still say someone is "touched" to convey madness.

Sufferers from tuberculosis, or, as it used to be known, consumption, had been led away by faeries night after night, although they had no memory of this nocturnal abduction. Victims of elf shot had invisible wounds that could cause them to sicken and die mysteriously. A person held in a state of illusion by a faerie spell could no longer perceive reality and often became obsessed by the lure of wealth or beauty.

A wicked faerie, full of rage, might spit in a human's eye and cause a squint or even blindness, while a specific look could cause the recipient to fall into a trance and lose all memory, or fall into a coma-like sleep.

Protective Measures

Around the world, people found ways to protect themselves from the dreadful powers of these supernatural beings. In Britain, carrying a hazel wand or a twig of rowan guarded

Ferdinand Lured by Ariel, *Sir John Everett Millais, 1849–50, oil on panel, The Makins Collection*

against faerie curses. Turning socks or pockets inside out was also effective. If night-time abductions were suspected, mortals could protect themselves by placing an iron under their beds or hanging a pin cushion stuck with pins behind their doors.

In Cambodia, people called upon good house faeries to protect them from the wicked ones. In France, flaxseed was spread on the floor to repel goblins—

Faerie Curses

To offend faeries brought many forms of ill luck to a home, and our ancestors had to be constantly on their guard to prevent this from happening. Evil faeries struck where they could do most harm, such as by causing crops to fail, or create most grief. Some particularly nasty faeries were known to seek out children in order to harm them. In Germany, for example, the pilwiz, evil goblin-like creatures with sickles on their big toes, would try to inflict hurt, and in West Africa, abiku would enter children's bodies, absorbing everything their hosts ate and drank until the children sickened and died.

some goblins are just crabby or mischievous but others are known to be downright wicked.

In Mexico, tobacco smoke was used to disperse bad faeries. In Trinidad, carrying a mirror protected against the sukuyan, a malevolent faerie who is frightened by her own reflection.

Sprite Traps

A magical device used to capture dangerous faeries, spirits, and ghosts, a sprite trap is made from a blackthorn stave and copper wire that has never carried electricity. During a ritual process, the copper wire is bound to the stave with red thread and the stave is marked with a Dag (or D) rune.

The trap is then set at the entrance to the home or other location where a malevolent faerie is causing disturbances. As a lure, a cleft blackthorn stave with a lighted candle is placed in front of the trap.

Once the faerie, or other spirit, is captured in the sprite trap, it is taken to a remote place and the red thread cut with a consecrated knife. The thread is then placed into a witch bottle that has been prepared to imprison the faerie. A spell is recited while the thread is placed into the bottle, which is corked and sealed with red wax before being buried. A thorn bush is planted on the site.

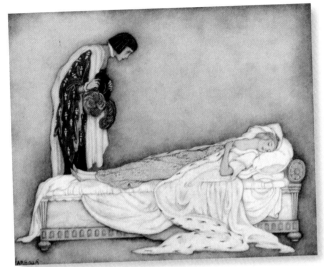

The Prince looks down on Sleeping Beauty, *Jennie Harbour*

If the witch's bottle containing the faerie is found and opened, a very angry faerie quickly escapes.

The Spell of Sleep

Some mortals hate to believe there is really such a thing as a wicked faerie who is truly bad through and through. Such optimists about faerie nature point to the wicked faerie in *Sleeping Beauty*, who is enraged at having been left out of the christening feast. Although her seemingly evil spell is meant to cause the death of the princess, it ultimately leads to her marriage to a handsome prince.

Although the princess in *Sleeping Beauty* sleeps for a hundred years thanks to a benevolent spell that saves her from death, faeries could condemn a mortal to a state of sleep that keeps the victim in eternal limbo, neither dead nor truly alive, simply out of curiosity. Beautiful brides, because they are fascinating to faeries, were once especially likely to suffer this fate.

The Stolen Bride

In Irish faerie lore, red-haired men are considered lucky and often appear as the means of rescue by which mortals are released from the power of faeries.

About the year 1670, a personable young man with auburn hair lived in County Clare. He was brave and strong, and he had his own land with no one to lord it over him. There was nothing he liked more than to take a stroll around his estate at twilight, looking at the sun setting below the trees.

One frosty November Eve he saw a dark mass moving along the edge of the river that separated his land from the wilderness beyond. He watched and waited till the black mass came closer, then he distinctly perceived that it was a troop of faeries carrying a bier on their shoulders, on which lay a corpse covered with a white cloth. They laid it down, apparently to rest themselves.

Curiosity got the better of the young man and he fired a bullet from his gun above their heads. The faeries vanished in a moment, leaving the corpse alone on the bier. With trepidation the young man made his way to it and lifted the cloth where it covered the face. By the freezing starlight, he beheld the form of a beautiful young girl in her wedding dress, apparently not dead but in a deep sleep.

He raised her from the bier and carried her to his house where for twelve months she remained like one in a coma, yet unchanged, though she never tasted food for all that time.

When the next November Eve came round, he resolved to visit the spot by the river again, and watch from the same place in the hope of meeting with some adventure that might throw light on the history of the beautiful girl. His way lay beside the old ruined fort called Lios-na-Fallainge, the Fort of the Mantle, and as he passed, the sound of music and mirth fell on his ear. He stopped to catch the words that were being spoken, and did not have long to wait when he heard a low whisper.

The young man spoon-feeds the unconscious girl

"Wherever we go, I hope better luck will be ours than we had this night twelve months ago when we carried off a rich prize only to have it snatched from us."

"Yet," said another, "little pleasure has he had of his bride, for she has not eaten or drunk or uttered a word since she entered his house. And so she will remain until he makes her eat off her father's table-cloth, which covered her as she lay on the bier."

On hearing this, the young man rushed home and, without even waiting for the morning, entered the girl's room, took down the table-cloth, spread it across the bed and laid on it some morsels of food. Carefully, he spooned a tiny amount into her mouth as she slept. Immediately, she opened her eyes, choked, and swallowed.

This was the girl's story as she told it to the young man. She was to have been married to a young lord of her own county, and the wedding guests had all assembled when she felt ill suddenly and swooned away. Until the moment the food had touched her tongue she knew no more of what had happened, for the Spell of Sleep was upon her.

The young man escorted the girl home to her father, whose joy at beholding her was beyond words. So impressed with the young man were the girl and her father that they soon all came to agree that it would be best if she married him. The wedded pair lived together happily for many long years after, and no evil befell them for the faeries had decided to let them be.

The Evil Eye

The influence of the mysterious and malign power of the Evil Eye used to be dreaded in all countries of the world. Anyone who is young, beautiful, talented, or special in any way, and naturally attracts attention and admiration, is open to the fatal blight that follows the glance of the Evil Eye. Although given by envious mortals, the Evil Eye cuts a channel through to an individual, making him or her vulnerable to the attentions of malevolent faeries. This is why it became the habit of rural people in past times never to praise anyone without adding instantly "God bless him/her," for, if this vital phrase were to be omitted, the worst consequences would befall the person praised.

By law, severe measures were once ordained against users of the malign influence. The Evil Eye acts like a malicious spirit, radiating a poisonous atmosphere that chills and blights its object. Many have felt that there is such a power and succumbed to its hold in a helpless, passive way, as if all self-trust and self-reliant energy were utterly paralyzed by its weight.

People thought to possess the power were held in great trepidation, and attractive children were kept out of their path. If a child fell sick, someone was immediately suspected of having omitted the saving invocation, "God bless it!" out of ill will. Nothing was more feared than the full, fixed, direct glance of one believed to wield the Evil Eye. If it fell upon a person, or on any of their household, a terrible fear and trembling of heart would overtake them, which

Baby Snatchers

Terrifying stories of faeries stealing newborn babies and leaving changelings in their place exist around the world. In Armenia, the als were the culprits. They would take babies, or blind them. In Japan it was wicked goblins, called bakemo, whilst in Malaysia babies were snatched by bajang, shape-shifting faeries who often took the form of a polecat. Devs took babies in Persia, and left changelings in their beds.

often led to sickness or sometimes even to death.

To undo the effects of the Evil Eye, a piece of the garment worn by the Evil-Eyed must be burned to tinder and ground to powder, then breathed in by the victim, whose forehead must be anointed with spittle three times. The Ancient Greeks, for example, lost no time in spitting three times in the face of the Evil-Eyed to break the spell.

The Changeling

Another reason to fear faeries was their habit of stealing attractive babies and leaving a changeling in place of the real infant. The changeling was a shape-shifting faerie in the form of the child, who would then appear to sicken and die. Alternatively, the changeling would be a demanding creature with a voracious appetite. The real child was held captive in Faerie.

To guard against this fate, people were careful never to mention a baby's good looks. For his or her protection, they would not only call God's blessing upon the child but spit at it, hoping this would make the faeries think the baby wasn't worth stealing. Baby boys were at most risk and so people would often dress them like girls for the first years, to deceive the faeries. In Britain, midwives blessed newborn babies with three drops of water—one for peace, one for wisdom, and one for purity. They might also make a cross with rowan twigs and hang it over the cradle to repel the evil intentions of bad faeries.

Even adults could be kidnapped—an adult changeling was recognizable by its harsh voice and mean-spirited personality.

Faeries around a baby's cot, *Warwick Goble, illustration to* The Book of Faerie Poetry *published 1920*

PART TWO

Faerie Havens

The overlap between the mortal world and the world of Faerie is particularly pronounced in the Celtic lands of Scotland, Cornwall, Wales, Ireland, and the Isle of Man. Secrets of the ancient wisdom that governs links between the visible and the unseen worlds are thought to lie in these places, and the wilder parts are renowned for being inhabited by faeries.

Midsummer Eve, *Edward Robert Hughes, watercolor*

Belief in Faeries

Through the centuries, tales from faerie lore relate ways in which these energetic sprites meddle in human affairs or punish people for trespassing into their world. Humans have been in turn afraid of faeries and enchanted by them. Such is the contrary and magical world of Faerie.

Belief in supernatural, invisible beings is almost universal. Stories of the extraordinary events that have unfolded when the world of Faerie crosses that of the mortal world reach as far back as the eighth and ninth centuries.

Sprites

In faerie lore, faeries of nature are often referred to as sprites. The word sprite originates from the Latin "spiritus," meaning spirit. Variations on the term include "spright," from which comes "sprightly"—meaning spirited or lively. Centuries ago in Europe, elves were sometimes known as sprites.

From medieval times onwards, faeries became a popular subject in western literature and it is in this period that the term "faerie" became common. Yet, even when different names were used to describe these creatures—not like mortals but not god-like either—there were faeries, and the places where they lived were treated with respect. In Ancient Greece, they were nymphs while Arabic people recounted tales of the jinn. In America, Innuit people and native Americans lived in a world they believed to be populated by powerful, unearthly forces. There is no race that has not believed, at one time or another, that the

Earth is inhabited by spiritual beings, who have their own energies and are not normally visible to human eyes.

Today our vision of faeries tends to be that they are pretty, harmless creatures, and for many sceptics they do not exist at all. This was not so for our ancestors. Sinister tales proliferated of the powerful magic of the faerie folk, and were narrated through the centuries as part of a strong oral tradition. Children grew up in awe of the invisible spirits with whom they shared their world, and as adults took care to appease them. The faeries of the past were feared as dangerous and powerful creatures, who might be friendly and helpful to humans, but could also be mischievous and even cruel.

Faerie Names

Through the centuries, faeries have been referred to using different synonyms and euphemisms, many of which were designed to mollify them and win their approval—perhaps with the wishful thought that, if they were named nicely, they would behave nicely too. These are some of the names given to faeries by those who wished to avoid falling out of favor with them. Most reflect the trepidation with which faeries were regarded and a desire to placate them with flattery:

Little folk or good folk

Good neighbors

Honest folk

Mother's blessing

The gentry

The people of peace

Green men

The lordly ones

A Native American tree faerie

Nymphs—Faeries of the Ancient World

Way back in antiquity, people believed in supernatural beings who were not gods, nor human, but revered as spirits of nature. The Ancient Greeks called them nymphs—we would call them faeries.

The name "nymph" comes from a Greek word meaning "young woman"—nymphs were always female and were perceived as caught eternally on the cusp between childhood and becoming a woman. Changeover times are always associated with the Middle Kingdom of Faerie.

Artists represented nymphs as gentle, loving, often musical creatures. They were believed to be the guardians of every natural living thing, from plants and trees to moors, bogs, rivers, streams, and mountains. Every one of these had its own, relatively benevolent faerie, working to keep it strong and healthy. These faeries were responsible for the harmonies of nature and for channeling energy, or life force, through all living things.

Tree Nymphs

Although tree nymphs are sometimes thought to be androgenous, they are usually perceived as female. Shy faeries, they seldom venture more than a few feet away from their tree and are rarely seen, although the odd sighting of a nymph in a tree's hollow has been reported, when the moon is full.

It was thought that nymphs were especially likely to inhabit the trees of deep, mysterious forests, and their lives were believed to begin and end with that of a particular tree. Writers and artists of the time often depicted tree nymphs as being pursued by their male counterparts, the satyrs.

Tree nymphs may be reticent but they are occasionally mischievous and have been known to play tricks on people. Guardians of trees, groves, and forests, they do not mean any harm, however, except when a human has damaged their charge. Then they deal as severe a punishment as is within their power. In a forest, a number of weapons can be wielded against mortals—branches can be blown suddenly to hit heads and faces, brambles can be tied around ankles, and thorns and sharp twigs can pierce skin.

Mostly, though, the nymphs of the woodland are gentle, soulful beings, who have such bewitching singing voices that a traveler journeying through the forest

The Dryad, *Evelyn De Morgan, 1884-85, oil on panel*

can lose all sense of time. If you are in a secluded spot, particularly among oak trees, you are likely to be surrounded by woodland nymphs. Those occupying an entire grove are the Alseid Glen, but they have different names, depending on the tree they inhabit: Daphnai, laurel; Dryad, oak or willow; Epimeliad, apple; Leuce, poplar; Melia, ash.

Land Nymphs

These faeries were linked to natural features of the landscape. Mountain vales and pastures were guarded by the auloniad; the helead looked after fenland; the hesperide were found in gardens; caves and underground tunnels were home to the lampade; the leimoniad lived in meadows, the napaeae/naphae in wooded valleys, and the oreiad in grottoes and mountains.

The Sad Story of Echo

An oreiad nymph of Mount Kithairon in Boiotia, Echo was cursed by the goddess Hera for distracting her with chatter. As punishment, Echo could only repeat the

Watery Places

Every type of water has its resident guardian nymphs:

Fountains	Crinaeae
Marshes	Eleionomae
Fresh-water	Limnade
Flowing water	Naiads
Clouds	Nephelads
Sea	Nereids
Oceans	Oceanids
Springs	Pegaeae
Rivers and streams	Potameide

last words of something just spoken. Although pursued by the god Pan, Echo fell in love with a beautiful boy— Narcissus. When he spurned her advances, she pined and faded away, leaving only her echoing voice behind. On vases, Ancient Greek painters depicted Echo as a winged nymph, her face shrouded by a veil.

Water Nymphs

Their penchant for luring handsome young men to a watery grave has given water nymphs a bad reputation. The naiads, for example, although mainly benign faeries, ensnared a young mortal, Hylas, who had come near to draw water, and he was never seen again.

Shape-shifting Magic

The nymph Arethusa, a companion of the goddess Artemis, loved to wander freely, enjoying the beauty of nature. One day, tempted by the promise of a bathe, she dived into a cool stream. The god of the river, Alpheus, became deeply fascinated by her but, like Artemis, Arethusa preferred to remain chaste and so she fled his advances. Undeterred, he took the form of a hunter, chasing her over the sea to Sicily. Finally, Arethusa found refuge on the island of Ortygia, near Syracuse, where she called upon Artemis to rescue her. Artemis responded to her plea by transforming the nymph into a sparkling spring.

Hylas and the Nymphs, *John William Waterhouse, 1896, oil on canvas*

Ireland's Faeries

In the Emerald Isle, westerly winds carry a whisper of other-worldly voices, and an ever-present sense of the supernatural pervades the landscape. Faerie dwellings, which are sometimes called "gentle" places, include mysterious earthen burial mounds, sea caves, sunken grassy pathways, deep lakes, and even a solitary blackthorn bush.

In the 1940s, Irish writer Sean O'Faolain recounted how a Cork woman had been asked whether she believed in faeries. "I do not," she replied after pondering the question, "but they're there."

Electricity didn't illuminate the rural west until the 1950s, and many older people remember gloomy winter evenings in the local "rambling house." Here folk gathered to sing the old songs and hear the seannachie (shan-a-key) tell wondrous stories

"Ireland is a land of mists and mystic shadows; of cloud-wraiths on the purple mountains; of weird silences in the lonely hills, and fitful skies of deepest gloom alternating with gorgeous sunset splendours."

Lady Francesca Wilde

of events that befell mortals on the high days of the old Celtic calendar—May Eve, Midsummer's Eve and Hallowe'en—when the gateway between our world and that

The Lakes and Mountains of Killarney, Ireland, *attr. to Jonathan Fisher*

of Faerie flies open. Doomed love affairs between mortal men and faerie women were described by the seannachie, as were the antics of the shape-changing púca (see page 134), the crafty leprechaun (see page 112), and web-footed merrows (see page 47), who hoarded the souls of drowned fishermen inside lobster pots.

The Perilous Realm

In Irish faerie lore, the Faerie island, Tir-na-n'Og (the Perilous Realm), shimmering on the Atlantic horizon for one day every seven years, provided a rich diversity of fantastic tales. This Faerie realm could sometimes be glimpsed in the depths of a lake or down wells, as well as beneath the ocean. Ancient myths tell of the bard Oisin (o-sheen) being taken to Tir-na-n'Og by his faerie lover, Niamh (neeve). Pining for his companions, Oisin returns to find his comrades all dead and forgotten. The moment his foot touches Irish soil, he ages by 300 years.

An entrance to Tir-na-n'Og may be found in Lough Gur in County Limerick, a magical place. The lake has collected within a circle of low-lying hills, but once every seven years it appears as dry land, and this is when the entrance is exposed. Every lake in Ireland has a guardian sidhe (shee), one of the ancient faerie race. The guardian of Lough Gur is known as Toice Bhrean (cho-ik-brain), the Lazy One, because she neglected to watch over the well, from which the lake sprang forth. It is believed that once every seven years a mortal meets his death by drowning in the lake—taken by the Bean-Fionn, the White Lady (see pages 45–6.)

The Gentry

The social order of the sidhe is thought to parallel that of the old aristocracy of Irish families, which is in itself a reflection of the ancient Celtic caste system. Due to their tall, noble appearance and silvery sweet speech, the sidhe are often known simply as "the Gentry." Their country is Tir-na-n'Og where they live a life of perpetual youth and beauty, never knowing disease or death, which is not to come on them till Judgment Day. Then,

unlike mortals, who are promised immortality, the sidhe are fated to pass into annihilation and be seen no more.

Origins of the Sidhe

Many tales of the seannachie revolved around the sidhe, who are air-element faeries, sometimes thought to have evolved from the Tuatha Dé Danann (too-a-de-danan). These were the peoples of the goddess Dana, and inhabited Ireland before humankind arrived in the form of the Gaels, sons of Mil, also known as Milesians. The Gaels battled the Tuatha Dé Danann and forced a vast number of them to flee Ireland. Those who elected to stay, led by Finvarra, their king, retreated underground to live in hollow hills—this is why the sidhe are also sometimes referred to as the "people of

The Gentry

Body Swap

Every seven years, according to Irish faerie lore, the faeries are obliged to deliver up a sacrifice to the Prince of Darkness. To save their own people, they try to abduct some beautiful young mortal girl, and hand her over instead.

the mounds"—where they built great cities. Equipped with supernatural powers, some of these beings continue to seek vengeance by tormenting mortals who live above ground.

A different version of the origins of the sidhe is that they were once angels in Heaven, but were cast out as a punishment for their pride. Some fell to Earth, some were cast into the sea, while others were seized by demons and dragged down to Hell from where they rise as evil faeries to tempt men to destruction.

Chief among their disguises is that of a beautiful young maiden endowed with the power of song and gifted with bewitching wiles. Under the influence of these sirens, a man will commit any and every crime. Once his soul is utterly black, the malign faeries carry him down to Hell.

Sad Fate

In ancient Ireland, a great faerie chief asked Saint Columb if there was any hope left to the sidhe that one day they would regain Heaven and be restored to their place among the angels. When the saint answered that there was no hope, the doom of the sidhe was fixed, for so had it been decreed by the justice of God, and the faerie chief fell into melancholy. He and his court sailed away from Ireland, to await the coming of the terrible Judgment Day when the faerie race is to disappear from Earth.

Without hope of regaining Heaven, on Judgment Day the sidhe are destined to perish utterly while humans are to be given immortality. The knowledge that the beautiful faerie race is doomed darkens the lives of the sidhe with a mournful envy of humanity.

The Faerie King

Faerie King and Queen

Finvarra—who is variously called Finvara, Finn Bheara, Finbeara, and Fionnbharr—became High King of the sidhe who chose to stay in Ireland. In some legends of faerie lore, he is also the King of the Dead. Finvarra is a benevolent figure who ensures good harvests, strong horses, and great riches to those who assist him. However, he is also a womanizer, who frequently kidnaps mortal women. In County Galway a ruin stands on the faerie hill of Knockma. This

is "Finvarra's Castle" beneath which is said to lie the palace and court of the king of the Irish faeries. Finvarra's Castle is mentioned in manuscripts stretching back many centuries.

All the sidhe women are lovely to behold with long golden hair that sweeps the ground. Onagh, the Faerie Queen, is most beautiful of all; she is robed in silver gossamer that sparkles with diamonds like dew drops. The Queen is more spellbinding than any woman on earth, yet Finvarra spends much of his time dancing with, and seducing, mortal women, whom he lures to his faerie palace with enchanting music. Those he keeps are mourned as dead by friends and family, although they are leading a joyous life in a beautiful faerie palace in the heart of the hills. Others dance all night with Finvarra, yet in the morning are found fast asleep in bed. With memories of all they have heard and seen, however, these young women know the art of secret love potions, by which they can work spells over those whose love they desire.

Faerie Palaces

The faeries of Irish lore are much more numerous than mortals. In their palaces, called sifra, in the hollow hills and under the sea, they hide away many treasures. All the wealth of wrecked ships is theirs, and all the riches that mortals have buried in the earth when danger was upon them, dying before they could reclaim it. Once all the precious metals of the mines and the jewels of the rocks belonged to faeries, too. In the sifra, crystal walls and floors are bejeweled with pearls, and the banquet-hall is lit by the glitter of diamonds that stud the rocks. To find the sifra's entrance, all a mortal need do is walk nine times around a hollow hill, or faerie rath, at the full moon.

Seelie and Unseelie Courts

In Irish and Scottish faerie lore, faeries are part of the Seelie (blessed or holy) Court, presided over by Finvarra, or the Unseelie (unholy) Court, according to their nature. The sidhe of the Seelie Court are fairly beneficent toward mortals, returning kindnesses with favors of their own, though they also avenge perceived insults and are prone to mischief. They

A faerie palace

are most likely to be seen by mortals at twilight, walking on the ground as the sun sets.

The Unseelie Court consists of malevolent, wickedly inclined faeries, who form a faerie host called the Sluagh Sidhe (sluagh means "host" or "army"). No offense is necessary to attract the attention of the Sluagh Sidhe, who travel through the air at night, assaulting travelers and even trying to snatch sleeping mortals from their beds.

The Faerie Host

In 1972 the Irish Folklore Commission found villagers around Lough Gur who still spoke of the Wild Hunt, sometimes called the Dead Hunt. Phantom dogs,

Vampiric Enchantress

The Leanhaun Sidhe is a beguiling faerie woman, an enchantress who seeks the love of mortal men. Sometimes described as the Celtic Muse, she targets poets and other creative men, vampirically feeding on their life-force until they waste away.

heard but never seen, chased their invisible quarry from this world to the next. It was suggested that only older people could hear the hunt; the following day inevitably brought them news of a local death. The Sluagh Sidhe form a part of the Wild Hunt, along with restless spirits of the dead. Also referred to as the Marcra Sidhe, or faerie cavalcade, the faerie host are especially likely to be present at midnight above mortal homes, and these fearsome faeries are known to take captured mortals with them on their journeys.

Coming from the West, the Sluagh Sidhe fly in groups like flocks of birds and attempt to enter a house where someone is dying to take that person's soul away with them. West-facing windows are sometimes kept closed to keep them out.

At the Cave of Cruachan in County Connaught stands the Hell Gate. Once a year, at Hallowe'en, the gate opens and the Wild Hunt rides forth accompanied by the Cu Sidhe, the hell hounds, and a flock of copper red birds that ruin crops with their poisonous breath. For mortals to travel alone at night at this time was considered to be extremely dangerous—everyone had to be especially careful to guard against such monstrosities, which might try to attack them.

The Dearg-Dur is Ireland's legendary vampire, one of the undead who consort with faeries. In some tales, the Dearg-Dur takes the shape of a pale young woman who lingers in graveyards at night waiting for unwary passers-by. Her beauty is irresistibly seductive, but when she kisses, she feeds on blood, draining the life from her victim.

Mortal Defenses

Irish faerie lore abounds with clever ways for people to defend themselves from the wrath of envious and dispossessed faeries. For example, mortals walking at night would bring along a piece of glowing coal or turf stuck on a stake or a fork to serve as a weapon. Fleeing into a graveyard or jumping across a creek were other options, because it was believed the sidhe couldn't follow you into consecrated ground or across water.

An evil faerie

Twisted stalks of straw, about six inches long, were dipped into holy water and the resulting "deisréad" (desh-raid) was carried in an outstretched hand to ward off malignant faeries.

The four-leaved shamrock, a motif of good luck, is still thought to guard against faerie bewitchments.

Never insult the Sidhe

Sometimes referred to in placatory terms as "the good people," the sidhe had the power to bring prosperity to a farm—or, conversely, to withhold their favors. If neglected, the sidhe could prove spiteful. Thanks to pishogues (pish-oge)—faerie spells—hens refused to lay eggs, milk went sour, and livestock wandered astray. Farmers and cattle alike would sicken if struck by faerie darts, tiny Neolithic arrowheads that continue to be found today. Accidents and untimely deaths were proof that the sidhe had been badly slighted in some way.

A grievous insult to the sidhe was to build a new house across a faerie path (see pages 26–7). In Irish faerie lore, a lone tree growing in the middle of a sheepfold, beside a well, or on a hilltop is protected by the Lunanti Sidhe, guardian faeries of nature. The blackthorn is so sacred that not even dead branches should be removed. In 1891, W.B. Yeats wrote of two farmers killed by the sidhe for the crime of tearing up a blackthorn, the faerie thorn bush. The thorns are dangerous to mortals—a wound made by a thorn in a finger will go sceptic, and a thorn in the eye causes blindness.

Leprechauns

Perhaps the best known Irish faerie, the leprechaun is the faerie shoemaker, who tricks greedy mortals out of promised treasure, often by laying glamor (see page 20) on his gifts. Said to wear a rough red woollen coat and a hat, his original name in Irish is "lobaircin," meaning "small-

A leprechaun

bodied fellow." To seek out a leprechaun, look near ancient castles, where he is always engaged in making shoes, but usually just one—never a pair.

Self-appointed guardians of ancient treasure that has been buried in crocks or pots, leprechauns tend to avoid mortals, whom they regard as foolish and greedy. If caught, they take full advantage of this trait, as Tom Fitzpatrick, a farmer's son, would testify.

Tom, spying a leprechaun mending shoes behind a hedge, sidled up to him and grabbed him firmly, never taking his eyes off him—if you take your eyes off a leprechaun, he vanishes like smoke. To discover the whereabouts of the gold, Tom employed dire threats until the leprechaun showed him a vast field of yellow ragwort plants, and pointed out the particular flower under which the treasure lay. Tom marked the plant by tying a red garter around its stalk, and forgetting warnings about faerie trickery, unwisely released the leprechaun and ran home to fetch a spade. When he got back he found every ragwort in the field tied with red garters. Tom's prospects of riches had vanished with the leprechaun.

The Leprechaun's Relatives

The Fear Darrig, or Red Man, is a near relation of the leprechaun. He dresses in red—the color of magic—from head to toe. The faerie world's malevolent practical joker, the Fear Darrig is much amused by mortal terror and is known to give his victims terrifying nightmares. However, if in a good mood, the silver-tongued scoundrel can help to release captive mortals from the land of Faerie.

Another relative, the Cluricaun, is a troublesome household faerie with a penchant for raiding larders and wine cellars. On moonlit nights, he enjoys drunken sprees through the countryside, and may steal or borrow almost anything, creating mayhem in people's houses during the hours of darkness.

The Banshee

The Bean-Sidhe (ban-shee) forewarns members of certain ancient Irish families of their time of death. Weeping and wailing, she haunts just five families of the high Milesian race—the O'Neills, the O'Briens, the O'Connors, the O'Gradys, and the Kavanaghs.

The Banshee may appear as a female member of the family who died young, or as a stately matron in fine clothes; at other times she is an ancient crone, seen wearing either a gray, hooded cloak or a winding sheet, or grave robe. She may be seen and heard lamenting at night, shrouded and crouching beneath trees, with her face veiled, or flying past in the moonlight, crying bitterly. Her hair is always long and streaming and her eyes fiery red from weeping. She may also be seen apparently washing the blood-stained clothes of those who are about to die. In this guise she is known as the Bean-Nighe—washer-woman.

Yet the Banshee is not restricted to the shape of a woman. She may also appear in the mortal world as an animal or bird. A hooded crow, stoat, hare, or weasel are those she favors—creatures associated with magic and witchcraft.

"I saw the banshee flying . . .", *Florence Harrison, 1912, illustration to* Elfin Song

Piercing Wail

Since the Banshee heralds the demise of those of authentic noble stock, it is with great dread that her piercing keening, or wailing, is heard. Her cry is mournful beyond all other sounds on earth. In some parts of Ireland she is referred to as the Bean Chaointe—keening woman—whose wail can be so piercing that it shatters glass.

The Dullahan

One of the most spectacular beings in the faerie realm, the Dullahan—or Far Dorocha, meaning "dark man"—is active in remote parts of Ireland. Around midnight on certain Irish festivals or feast days, this wild, black-robed horseman may be observed riding a black steed across the countryside.

The Dullahan is always headless but carries its head with it, either on the saddle-bow of its horse or in its upraised right hand. The Dullahan's head is the color and texture of stale dough or moldy cheese. A hideous, idiotic grin splits the face from ear to ear, and the eyes, which are small and black, dart about like flies. The entire head glows with the phosphorescence of decaying matter and this malignant faerie being may use it as a lantern to guide its way along the darkened laneways of the Irish countryside.

Possessed of supernatural sight, the Dullahan, by holding its severed head aloft, can see for vast distances, even on the darkest night. Using this power, it can spy the spirit of a dying person, no matter where he lies. The Dullahan thunders through the night, using a human spine as a whip. The horse sends out sparks and flames from its nostrils as it charges along.

In some parts of the country, such as County Tyrone, the Dullahan drives a black, coffin-topped coach known as the coach-a-bower, from the Irish "coiste bodhar," meaning "deaf" or "silent coach." This is drawn by six black horses along sunken green lanes, traveling so fast that it often sets the bushes along the sides of the road on fire. All gates fly open to let the coach through, no matter how firmly they are locked.

Summoning Souls

On each journey this much-feared faerie undertakes, its disembodied head is permitted to speak just once, and even then it only has the ability to call the name of the person whose death it heralds. If it stops its snorting horse before the door of a house, it will shout the name of the person about to die, drawing forth the soul at the call.

A seannachie from the Mourne Mountains in County Down, recounts: "I seen the Dullahan myself, stopping on the brow of the hill between Bryansford and Moneyscalp late one evening, just as the sun was setting. It held up its own head in its hand and I heard it call out a name. I put my hand across my ears in case the name was my own, so I couldn't hear what it said. When I looked again, it was gone. But shortly afterwards, there was a bad car accident on that very hill and a young man was killed. It had been his name that the Dullahan was calling."

Unlike the Banshee's, the Dullahan's call is a summoning of the soul of a dying person rather than a death warning.

Cornish Piskies and the Faeries of Wales

As in other Celtic countries, the faeries of Cornwall and Wales are neither wholly good nor wholly evil. While Cornwall especially is renowned for sightings of mermaids, other faeries abound here as well—most typically the pixies, known as piskies, and their troublesome relatives the spriggans.

West Country Pixies

Pixies are found in other Celtic countries but, other than Scotland, they are most common in the west country of England, where they delight in living in bogs. On Dartmoor, in Devon, to be "pixie-led" is to be in an enchanted or trance-like state—like being "away with the faeries."

The Cornish piskies have red hair and dress in moss, grass, and lichen. They are mischievous but not malevolent—for example, they are helpful to the elderly but will lead astray able-bodied travelers on wild moorland. Mortals often choose to avoid piskie haunts, which are thought to include old stone circles and barrows.

Mother's Blessing

In South Wales, faeries are mostly referred to as the Bendith Y Mamau, the mother's blessing. Bendith Y Mamau were particularly ready to steal small children and replace them with their own changelings, known as crimbils. It was thought that the faeries needed to improve their stock with mortal blood.

Spriggans

Athough closely related to mischievous piskies, spriggans have darker and more dangerous natures than their cousins. While piskies are cheerful and fun loving, spriggans are spiteful and carry out malicious tricks on mortals to torment them. One of their favorite misdeeds is to lead lonely travelers into swamps or near to dangerous and crumbling cliffs—a cruel habit they share with the Will o' the Wisp (see page 119). Spriggans also cause such misfortunes as blighted crops, bad weather, and illness, and they swap babies and small children for changelings.

Spriggans are grotesquely ugly with wizened features and crooked skinny bodies. They haunt lonely places, such as castle ruins, barrows, certain standing stones, and windswept crags.

Tylwyth Teg

The Tylwyth Teg faeries of Wales live with their king, Gwyn ap Nudd, in the Land of Enchantment, which is what the Welsh call the world of Faerie. This

A faerie of the Twlwyth Teg

lies within the hollow banks that overhang the deepest parts of lakes and rivers, especially where foxgloves grow. Mortals can follow them no farther than the water.

Tylwyth Teg means "Fair Family" and refers to the flowing fair hair of the women. Like other faeries, the females sometimes choose mortal husbands, but Welsh men who wed a faerie wife find that she always longs to return to her own people.

On nights when the moon is full, Tylwyth Teg celebrate a "noswaith lawen"—a merry night. At midnight the faeries rise out of the ground, from every bank and valley, and join hands to form circles. They sing and dance until cock-crow, at which time they vanish. On moonless nights they are apt to carry glow-worms to light their way. According to many stories, time in their

Jack O'Lantern, *Arthur Hughes, 1872, oil on canvas*

realm passes much slower than it does in ours, so that a day in the Land of Enchantment could be anything from a year to a hundred years in the mortal world. This difference could prove disastrous for any mortals returning from the world of Faerie.

Will o' the Wisp

Mysterious lights that lead travelers from well-trodden paths into treacherous marshes are believed to be carried by a Will o' the Wisp. Many stories surround these dangerous faeries. A man, traveling home late in the evening, told of seeing a bright light moving before him. Looking closer, he saw that the light was a lantern held by a "dusky little figure," which he followed for several miles. To his shock, he suddenly found himself standing on the edge of a great chasm with a roaring torrent of water rushing below him. At that moment the lantern carrier leapt across the fissure, raised the light over its head and let out a malicious laugh, after which it blew out the light, leaving the man far from home, standing in pitch darkness at the edge of a precipice.

In some areas, the Will o' the Wisp is said to be a guardian of treasure, leading any mortal brave enough to follow it to great riches. In others, this mysterious faerie was said to appear just where a tragedy was about to occur. The Will o' the Wisp also appears to light the path of mortal funeral processions.

Regional Will o' the Wisps

Faeries resembling Will o' the Wisp appear all around Britain. These are some of the best known:

Joan the Wad	Cornwall, Somerset
The Lantern Man	East Anglia
The Hobby Lantern	Hertfordshire, East Anglia
Peg-a-Lantern	Lancashire
Spunkies	Lowland Scotland
Will o' the Wikes	Norfolk
Jenny with the Lantern	North Yorkshire, Northumberland
Hinky Punk	Somerset, Devon
Will the Smith	Shropshire
Hobbedy's Lantern	Warwickshire, Gloucestershire
Jack a Lantern	the West Country
Pinket	Worcestershire

Will o' the Wisps are also called corpse candles—reflecting their association with graveyards and funeral processions—and Ignis Fatuus, which means "foolish fire" in Latin.

Scotland's Faeries

Around the stormy seas and craggy cliffs of Scottish coasts, within the country's untamed woodland, and inside human homes are found an eclectic variety of faeries. Even when people can neither see nor hear them, they are perceived to be ever present.

In Scotland, a variety of names are used to refer to faeries, including the Still Folk, People of Peace, the Silent Moving Folk, the Wee Folk, and Prowlies. The word for an air-element faerie is "sith," pronounced "shee," just as in the Irish sidhe. Also like the Irish faeries, sith live in hollow hills, from which spellbinding music permeates the night air, and they congregate in the Seelie and Unseelie Courts. As in Ireland, the Unseelie Court is thoroughly evil, and in Scotland people have described these faeries as forming a massive dark cloud that rides upon the night winds, and from which emanates an unnerving cackling and howling.

Earth Faeries

All over Scotland, earth faeries live alongside mortals, whether for good or ill. Household faeries, such as brownies (see pages 78–82), look for deserving homes, whose inhabitants are humble and gracious, but brownies do not like cats and will steer clear of places where they live. Brownies wear suits of green, blue, or brown with little felt caps, and for their own quarters, they like the attic, woodshed, or cellar of a mortal home best.

In the Shetland and Orkney Islands, other household faeries, the trows, are active at night. These round, legless faeries move about by rolling their bulbous forms, or bouncing like rubber balls, and they tend to hide things in odd places.

Gnomes, on the other hand, relatives of the brownies, live deep in ancient Scottish forests under old oak trees, where they make their dwellings among intricate root systems. Here, they are believed to be protective of wildlife and adept at the magical healing of sick or injured animals.

Buachailleen—small male faeries, which are sometimes known as "the herding boys"—are mischievous shape-shifters, most often seen in rural areas in summer wearing small red hats, which are sometimes inverted flower caps. Herds are protected from them by the Gruagach, also known as the herdswoman, who keeps the animals safe and leads them to water. A solitary female faerie, she wears a green gown and carries a shepherd's staff, but is

The Nymph, "Now Again She Flies Aloof,"
Thomas Cooper Gotch, watercolor on paper

grotesque in her appearance. Always cold, she loves to sit near a mortal fireside—hence her other name, the firesitter. If allowed to warm herself by the fire, she looks after home and herds in return. Highlanders still pour milk into hollow stones as offerings to her.

A less welcome faerie is the Fachan. He has just one of everything—one head, one eye, one ear, one arm, one leg, one foot, one toe, and so on, down the center of his face and body, which are both hairy

A heather faerie

possess sublime beauty. Trooping faeries who love dancing and music, their gatherings in northern England and Scotland are known as pixie fairs. Pixies dread iron, which kills them on contact. Their cousins, the heather pixies, are mischievous pranksters with delicate translucent wings. They live on heather moorland in the Scottish Lowlands.

and feathered. He carries a vicious spiked club, which he swings to chase away visitors from his home on top of the highest mountains in the Highlands.

Small, winged faeries with heads too large for their bodies, and small pointed ears and noses, are the pixies. They hold foxgloves and toadstools sacred, and like to wear parts of plants as garments. Pixies are most likely to be seen at Beltaine, and their tiny queen is said to

Tree Faeries

Dryads, tree-dwelling faeries from the ancient world, live in all Celtic countries, especially Scotland. They are most likely to be found in the faerie triad of oak, ash, and blackthorn, or of rowan, birch, and elder. Faerie willows that have dryads living in them are said to move about at night, seeking new locations to lay down roots while singing beautiful songs that entrance mortals.

People walking through enchanted woods must take care not to be grabbed by the long, green arms of the Ghillie

Dhu, which will drag them into the world of Faerie forever. Scottish forests were once heavily populated by these guardian tree faeries but they are now said to be rare—although since they are shape-shifting faeries and disguise themselves as foliage, it might be hard to tell. Ghillie Dhu are most active at night and prefer birch trees to all others, guarding them jealously from humans.

Water Faeries

Renowned for its lochs and rivers, and miles of remote coastline, islands and rocky shores, Scotland attracts a fascinating mix of water faeries. Ashrays, male and female, look like young mortals but are actually ancient. Their whitish skin is almost translucent and they are mainly active at night under water—they cannot live on land. If touched by sunlight they melt into a rainbow pool of water.

Faerie waterbirds are occasionally glimpsed along Scottish coasts. These are boobrie, about a foot high with black feathers, large, sharp-looking claws and an enormous three-foot bill. This water-bound faerie is mainly active at night, and is able to shape shift into a horse and gallop along the top of the water, giving sailors the impression that they have seen a ghost horse.

Although fin folk shun contact with mortals, they intend no harm, living beneath the lochs in their own underwater world, where they enjoy gardening in a paradise of flowers and lush foliage. They are also known as sea gardeners and the lady's own.

A solitary water faerie, the Ly Erg appears in the form of a small soldier who raises a red right hand—bloody as a

Bright-eyed Seals

The selkies of northern Scotland and the Isles are seal-like sea faeries who often come to dance on land, especially on the night of the full moon, shedding their sealskins and appearing as beautiful women with webbed hands and feet. If a mortal man hides a selkie's sealskin, she will pine until she finds it and can slip back beneath the waves, her true home.

result of those he has killed in combat—
to give mortals a portent of death. He can
be found on lonely roadsides near water.

Urisks also live near water, but in
isolated woodlands. They are intelligent,
benevolent faeries, but are so extremely
ugly, they have been blamed for
frightening mortals to death. They are
wrinkled and hairy in patches with duck
feathers on their backs and necks, and
their emaciated bodies are topped by
huge, misshapen heads.

Scottish coasts are notoriously home to
mermaids (see pages 48–51) but they are
also populated by a race of malevolent
sea faeries called the Blue Men of the
Muir. These much-dreaded creatures
cause storms in the North Sea and throw
boulders at passing ships.

Another set of ill-tempered sea faeries
are the nucklelavees (see pages 46–7),
who are native to the Hebridean Islands.
These foul-smelling creatures are half
human and half horse with fins as feet,
but they can take on any form they wish,
always choosing to appear to mortals in
as hideous a way as possible. They enjoy

Famous Green Ladies

The Green Lady of Skipness Castle, by Loch
Fyne, has protected the castle, as well as
the families who have lived there, for
centuries. On several occasions she has
created confusion among enemies
planning an attack. After they left
Skipness, their wits returned but as they
marched back toward the castle, they
became confused again.

Green ladies are not confined to Scotland.
In Caerphilly, just north of Cardiff in Wales,
a green lady disguises herself as ivy,
clinging to the walls of the ruined castle. If
a mortal watches very closely, she will
reveal her presence by moving slightly.
Once she knows she has been seen, she
will emerge graciously and extend a hand
in welcome before vanishing.

coming out of the sea and chasing
humans just to frighten them, and can
only be escaped by crossing over running
water, such as a creek or river.

Shellycoats dwell in shallow pools of
fresh water and in woodland lakes. Small
beings, shellycoats nevertheless have
huge mouths and eyes, giving them a
fish-like appearance. Usually dark red or

purple in color, they bob near the water's surface where mortals might catch a glimpse of their large eyes.

In the seas around Orkney and the Shetland Islands, uilbheist—multiheaded sea monsters from the world of Faerie— guard the inlets and rocky shore. Their purpose seems to be the protection of the islands, not the wilful destruction of ships. Perhaps they also protect the shopiltees, playful little faerie water-horses, seen only in these waters.

The Glaistig, the Green Lady

This solitary faerie of the Scottish Highlands has the upper half of a woman and the lower half of a goat. Long golden hair falls about her body and her skin is dusky or gray. She usually wears a long, flowing green robe to cover her lower body. Half a faerie of the earth element, half of the water element, her Gaelic name literally means "water imp." She wanders the lonely lochs and rivers, and is regarded as both benevolent and malevolent toward humans. It is said that she was once a mortal noblewoman who

was smitten by the faeries, and who was granted her wish to become one.

The Glaistig has been known, like the Banshee (see page 113), to wail at the death of significant mortals, yet she is also a trickster—throwing stones and leading travelers astray from their paths. She is a mischievous friend to children, as well as herder of domestic cattle or of wild deer. In the village of Ach-na-Creige on the Isle of Mull, for example, a Glaistig served as the guardian of the local cattle, and it was customary to pour some milk into a holed stone on the cattle fold as a gift to her. This small token was the only payment she requested for her long vigils.

The Glaistig

Manx Faeries

Once, the Isle of Man was inhabited only by faeries. A blue mist hung continually over the land, so sailors in passing ships did not suspect it was there. Keeping a perpetual fire going preserved the mist, but one day the fire went out and some fishermen discovered the shore.

Like the faeries of other Celtic lands, those on the Isle of Man—the mooinjer-veggey, meaning "Little People"—live in hollow hills, emerald green pastures betraying a supernatural presence. The interior of Faerie Hill, in Rushen, is the palace of the Faerie King, and many a tale is told of midnight revels held there, and of faerie parades across the island. Faeries also inhabit caves, rivers, and even some roads on the island, particularly where there are bridges or crossroads.

Some of the Manx faeries are benevolent, curing sick people and helping those in peril. Others are malevolent, abducting children and even adults, and bringing misfortune. Flint arrowheads, which have been picked up occasionally all over the island, are the weapons by which the little people avenge themselves upon mortals who

Glashtin

In the Isle of Man, stories are recounted about the island's water-horse faerie, the Glashtin. At Glen Meay, the glen below the waterfall is haunted by the spirit of a man who one day met the Glashtin and, thinking it was an ordinary horse, got up on its back. It rushed to the sea to drown its rider, whose restless spirit now haunts the glen.

Peel Harbour, with the Castle in the background, *A. Heaton Cooper, 1909, illustration to* Isle of Man

have wronged them. The arrows' impact is not felt, and does not break the skin, but a blue mark is found on the body of the victim after death.

Good Relations

An old custom was to keep a fire burning in the grate during the night, so that the faeries might come in and enjoy it. It was also customary to leave some bread out for them, and to fill the water crocks with clean water before going to bed. This water was not used for any other purpose, but was thrown out in the morning. Manx women did not spin on Saturday evenings because this was deemed displeasing to the faeries, and at every baking and churning small portions of dough and butter were fixed to the wall for the faeries to eat.

Besides keeping on good terms with benevolent faeries, Manx folk found ways to defeat the machinations of the malevolent ones. Among these were incantations and herbs obtained from faerie doctors, or charmers. To protect themselves from malevolent faeries on May Eve, islanders would hang a wooden cross bound with sheep's wool to the inside of their front doors.

If any household item were to be mislaid and then found somewhere unexpected, Manx people would say that a faerie had borrowed it and returned it. If a person fell over, others would say that a faerie had laid something in their path to trip them up as a punishment for some offense they had caused.

The Elfin Knight

It is said that an elfin knight spied a lovely mortal girl sitting beneath the blue tree of Glen Aldyn, and fell in love with her. Asking to abandon the faeries for a domestic life with the girl, he left the faerie court during the celebration of the Rehollys Vooar Yn Ouyr, or Royal High Harvest Festival, celebrated by the faeries with dancing in Glen Rushen. This offended the Faerie King so greatly that he cursed the knight with an undying existence on the Manx mountains in the form of a satyr. Transformed by this malevolent magic, the knight became a sad, solitary wanderer.

Careless Talk Costs Lives

It was particularly important for mortals not to talk about faeries incautiously when out of doors, for the wind would carry anything that was said to faerie ears, and terrible retribution could be the result. However, to be in favor with the faeries meant that seemingly impossible tasks could be accomplished, although such help might be dearly paid for.

To appease faeries for any annoyances they caused—it was well known, for instance, that faeries object greatly to noise made by mortals, especially to the ringing of church bells—people tried to remember to display good manners at all

The Fenoderee or Phynnodderee (there are several ways of spelling the name)

times. For example, if when traveling from Douglas to Castletown a person crossed the "Faerie Bridge," he or she would say "laa mie," meaning "good day," or wave to the faeries. Cautionary tales abounded as to the consequences of neglecting to do so.

Manx Specials

A large, hairy, shaggy elf, the Phynnodderee is a hard-working, helpful faerie, though bad-tempered. He carries out many chores for farmers, who must remember never to present him with a new set of clothes, because if they do, he will disappear.

The Moddeh Dhoo, a faerie, or phantom, black dog that is capable of frightening mortals to death, lives in Peel Castle. During the period when the castle was a fortress with its own garrison of soldiers, this hound was seen all too often.

The most terrifying of all the Manx faeries, however, is the Buggane, an evil hobgoblin covered in black hair, with tusks and a large red mouth. Known to tunnel underground, the Buggane can resemble a giant, hideous mole, although one that speaks to people on occasion. The Buggane always has a particular home, such as a waterfall, a forest, or an old ruin, where he remains unless disturbed. The most famous Buggane is the one associated with the roofless church of St Trinian's on the main road between Peel and Douglas. Each time the roof was renewed, the Buggane tore it off again, terrorizing all and sundry. To this day the church has no roof.

Faerie Hounds and Horses

Faerie dogs are among the most commonly sighted of all faeries, and they often appear to mortals at the crossover time between life and death—although unpredictable in nature, they can be kindly rescuers. Faerie horses, on the other hand, mostly seem to have evil intentions.

Faerie Dogs

Faerie dogs are frequently seen as fearsome beings foretelling death or disaster, despite some having friendlier traits. Some are shape shifters who can take the form of different animals, while others always appear in the same guise.

Hounds of Scotland and Wales

The Cu Sith hunts in the Scottish Highlands, mostly in complete silence, but it sometimes barks three times so piercingly that the sound travels for many miles. Although green is the color of the faeries, this faerie dog is the only one with green fur. Its coat is long and shaggy, and the dog is the size of a small calf. Not surprisingly, the Cu Sith was considered dangerous to meet. Their Irish equivalent is the Cu Sidhe, or hell hound.

Silent Listeners

It was once believed that domestic animals, especially the dog and the cat, know everything about their mortal owners. They listen to everything that is said, watch facial expressions, and can even read thoughts. The Irish once said it is not safe to ask a question of a dog, for it may answer, and should it do so, the questioner would surely die.

Another faerie dog to roam the Scottish countryside is Black Angus. A large dog with yellow eyes and sharp fangs, Black Angus appears to those who will die in a fortnight. To bring his dreadful message, Black Angus first crosses the path of the unlucky person, then springs out in front of them with a fearsome growl.

In Wales, where Annwn is the name for the underworld, the faerie hounds, Cwn Annwn, are also a portent of death. Their growling is loudest when they are at a distance but, as they draw near, it seems to grow softer and softer.

Padfoot

This shape-shifting faerie often appears in the form of a large black—though sometimes white—dog, or a black donkey, with large, glowing eyes. Padfoot can also be a supernatural sheep with shaggy fur and fiery red eyes, or just a bundle of wool rolling along the road. Sometimes visible, sometimes not, Padfoot pads eerily along behind or beside mortals, roaring or rattling chains, scaring them to death. The troublesome

The Hound of the Baskervilles,
Sidney Paget, 1901–2, illustration in The Strand Magazine

boggart (see page 82) sometimes takes the form of a padfoot but he is, on the whole, much friendlier than the more usual omen of death.

Skryker

The squelching sound of this faerie dog's walk gives it the nickname "Trash." It may walk invisibly alongside mortals, constantly moaning and howling, or it may be heard shrieking in the woods. When visible, Skryker is a huge faerie dog with vast paws and saucer eyes. Choosing to appear occasionally in front of lonely travelers, Skryker is an omen of impending misfortune. The worst thing a mortal can do is to try to hit Skryker, which brings instantaneous disaster or death.

Barguest

This shape-shifting faerie attaches itself to a particular area, where it serves as a warning of disaster or death to anyone who sees it, or to their family. The Barguest—also called Boguest or Barghest—takes many forms. It can be a large black mastiff with horns, fangs and fiery eyes; a huge shaggy-haired dog or bear with long sharp claws and glowing red eyes; a headless man or woman; or a white rabbit, cat, or dog that disappears in a burst of flames. Sometimes the Barguest is seen dragging chains, though it may also be wrapped in them. Any mortal who approaches the Barguest

Faerie or Phantom?

Church Grim, or Kirk Grim, is a supernatural black dog known to be the guardian of old churchyards, where it protects the dead from the devil and other demons. It was often seen on stormy nights and was regarded as a portent of death. However, Church Grim may well be a phantom rather than a faerie, due to the old Celtic practice of ensuring the first burial in a churchyard was that of a dog, who would watch over the rest of the dead.

receives horrible wounds that never heal. In common with many faeries, the Barguest cannot cross running water.

Black Dogs

Shape-shifting guardian faeries of ancient treasure or sacred ground take the form of huge shaggy-haired black dogs, about the size of a calf, with large eyes that glow a fiery red. They are usually encountered on secluded railroad tracks, ancient roads and crossroads, bridges, and in entranceways—the places of transition in mortal lives. Black dogs are usually harmless if left alone but any mortal trying to attack one will be punished with savage wounds, paralysis, or even death. Powerful faeries, black dogs can be either benevolent or fearsome toward mortals. Although the sight of one portends death within a year, they are well known for guiding to safety anyone who is lost, especially frightened women who are traveling alone.

Black Shuck

Also known as Shuck, Shuck Dog, or Old Shuck, this faerie dog displays similar behavior, and has a similar temperament, to black dogs. Black Shuck usually appears as an enormous shaggy black hound, the size of a donkey, with either two glowing red eyes or a single eye that emits a shower of red or green sparks. Black Shuck has also been seen in the form of a human monk with the head of a dog. Living in salt marshes and in the sea, it emerges at dusk to roam around marshes, roadways, river banks, and graveyards. Should it accompany a traveler, its presence can be felt in the touch of its shaggy coat and the brush of its icy breath. Black Shuck is harmless if left alone and deadly if challenged. In some areas, this faerie dog is enough to cause illness or death, in others it is a kind and helpful spirit, who will come to the defense of those who are being attacked and guide those who are lost.

Faerie Horses

Numerous witnesses report the existence of malignant faerie horses whose unnerving habits vary from taking unwilling mortals on hair-raising rides across the countryside to rushing into deep water, sometimes even drowning and devouring their captive riders. If

The Púca, *unnamed artist, 1862, in* Faerie Legends and Traditions *by Crofton Croker*

mortals make the mistake of touching or mounting an apparently harmless horse grazing at a lake side, they may be lucky to escape with their lives.

Púca, or Pookah

One of the most feared of all the shape-shifting faeries, the Púca, which is Irish for hobgoblin, can take many forms to wreak havoc on mortals. The Púca's favorite guise is that of a sleek, black horse with sulphurous yellow eyes and a long, wild mane. In this form, it roams large areas of countryside at night, tearing down fences and gates, scattering livestock in terror, trampling crops, and doing damage around remote farms. However, it may transform into a bull, goat, dog, bird, or bat. As a horse or calf, the Púca rushes between a mortal's legs and hoists its victim aboard for a mad dash across the countryside. This terrifying ordeal ends only when the rider is dumped in a ditch. In the shape of a bird or bat, the Púca flies low over mortals to scratch their faces. This malignant faerie lies in wait at deserted places of transition, such as a crossroads, a fence, or a bridge. Children were told not to eat blackberries once the seeds appear as this was a sign that the Púca had spat on them.

In some areas, though, the Púca is actually a helpful faerie, making prophecies and warnings. For example, according to a witness, a "plump, sleek, terrible steed" emerged from a hill in Leinster and spoke in a human voice to the people there on the first day of November. It gave "intelligent and proper answers to those who consulted it concerning all that would befall them until November the next year. And the people used to leave gifts and presents at the hill . . ."

The Kelpie

Lurking in and around the rivers and lochs of Scotland and Ireland, the Kelpie usually has grayish white fur. It may appear to be a lost pony, but its constantly dripping mane gives it away. The skin of this faerie water-horse is like that of a seal, only deathly cold to the

Unicorns

Not all faerie horses are malevolent. These gentle, magical creatures are known to be solitary and are most likely to be spotted in woodland at midnight, wandering beneath the stars under a canopy of dark oak trees. Milky white, with a silver mane and tail, the unicorn appears suddenly with no sound of hooves. When the creature moves its head, moonlight runs like seawater along the spiral of its pearly horn. It can disappear in the blink of an eye.

In faerie lore, the spiralled horn of the unicorn was called the 'alicorn' and has the power to detoxify poisons. Unicorns must keep their presence in the world a secret, otherwise they are hunted for their horns, which are said to protect mortals against diseases. If a unicorn horn is made into a cup, then no poison added to the drink it holds will take effect.

The Lady and the Unicorn: "Sight," *French School, 15th century, tapestry*

touch. Standing seemingly meek to let mortals mount it, the Kelpie loses no time in rushing into the water with them.

The Each Uisge

In Scotland, this faerie horse is much more dangerous than the Kelpie is in Ireland. It lures mortals in the same way, by standing near to the edge of seas and lochs to wait for someone to approach it. Once it has a rider, it sets off immediately for the deepest part of the water. It is impossible for mortals to free themselves because they become stuck to its adhesive supernatural skin. The Each Uisge (ech-ooshkya) drowns its rider, then devours the body, leaving only the liver.

Fictional Faeries

Faeries have so captured our imaginations that it is not surprising they appear in some of the world's best-loved books—or that they were once the subject of a creative hoax perpetrated by two fanciful and resourceful young girls.

Tinkerbell

In 1904, J.M. Barrie's play "Peter Pan, Or The Boy Who Wouldn't Grow Up," was staged, followed a few years later by a book, *Peter Pan and Wendy*, which featured a faerie called Tinker Bell, or Tinkerbell as she is better known these days. Possessing the variable faerie nature, she is sometimes spiteful but loves Peter Pan, her companion in Neverland. In the book, Tinker Bell's capriciousness is deemed to be because her tiny size prevents her from holding more than one feeling at a time. She is described as "exquisitely gowned in a skeleton leaf, cut low and square, through which her figure could be seen to the best advantage." This reflects how, in the popular imagination of modern times, faeries are seen mainly as tiny, beautiful, air-element females.

Tinker Bell is described as a common faerie who mends pots and kettles—a tinker—and is often referred to simply as "Tink." Tinker Bell can make it possible for others to fly, by sprinkling them with faerie dust, although mortals must believe for the dust to work its magic.

Flower Faeries

The illustrator Cicely Mary Barker (1895–1973) created the famous Flower Faeries. These tiny nature faeries—the tallest is only 4in (10cm)—are associated with a particular plant or tree, which they are responsible for looking after. They live and sleep in their flowers. To encourage their plants to grow, they tend and water them. Each faerie wears garments made from their own leaves and flowers. Like all faeries, they enjoy singing and dancing. Flower Faeries live in the garden as well as in wilder places, by the wayside, or in woodland. Within the woodland that is home to many of the Flower Faeries, the Bluebell faerie is king and Primrose is his queen. Other Flower Faeries, such as Buttercup and Daisy, are the particular friends of children.

Tinkerbell, *Nadir Quinto, from* Peter Pan and Wendy

The Cottingley Faeries

In 1917 in Yorkshire, two girls—Elsie Wright, aged 16, and her cousin 10-year-old Frances Griffiths—produced some photographs of faeries that were to become possibly the most famous of all faerie pictures.

Elsie and Frances used a simple camera, and their family confirmed that they lacked any knowledge of photography or photographic trickery. After the first photographs, another three years passed before the girls took three more pictures of their nature faeries. Although they said they could not photograph the faeries when anyone else was watching, they did have one independent witness, Geoffrey L. Hodson, a writer, who claimed to have seen the faeries and confirmed the girls' observations "in all details."

How the Story Unfolded

Family and friends teased Elsie and Frances about their story of seeing faeries near Cottingley Beck until, one day, Elsie borrowed her father's camera and, after some basic instruction on how to use it, walked to the woodland behind her family home to take photographs by the beck. When, that evening, Arthur Wright and Elsie developed the photographic plate in the dark room, it was to discover the captured image of a faerie. A second photograph showing a faerie resulted in the girls being banned from borrowing the camera again. The photographs were put in a drawer by Arthur Wright, who considered them to be pranks, although Elsie's mother was

Photographs of the Cottingley Faeries

convinced of their authenticity.

In 1918 Frances wrote to her friend Johanna Parvin in South Africa and enclosed a copy of one of the photographs. On the back of it she had written: "Elsie and I are friendly with the beck faeries. Funny, I never used to see them in Africa. It must be too hot for them there."

In her letter, Frances told her friend a variety of news, seeming more interested in the events of World War I and her favorite dolls than in the faeries, which are described in a matter-of-fact tone:

"... all think the war will be over in a few days, we are going to get our flags to hang up in our bedroom. I am sending you two photos, both of me, one is me in a bathing costume in our back yard, Uncle Arthur took that, while the other is me with some faeries up the beck, Elsie took that one. Rosebud is as fat as ever and I have made her some new clothes. How are Teddy and dolly?"

A Compelling Mystery

The debate over the authenticity of the photographs persisted for many years. Even those who do not believe that the photographs are of real faeries were compelled to question how—and why—they were made. In 1975, when the cousins were interviewed for a BBC broadcast, they did not give way to allegations that the photographs were tricks. Elsie gave an interesting answer that points to a realm in which fantasy and reality meet. She said: "I've told you that they're photographs of figments of our imagination and that's what I'm sticking to."

PART THREE

Finding Faeries

You can find faeries outside or in if you know where to look and what to do. So if your appetite has been whetted, and you decide that sharing your days with one of these spiritual beings is right for you, read on. One thing is for sure, faeries can add an extra dimension to your life, for good or ill.

"Take the Fair Face of Woman, and Gently Suspending, With Butterflies, Flowers, and Jewels Attending, Thus Your Faerie is Made of Most Beautiful Things" (Charles Ede), *Sophie Anderson*

A Walk in the Bluebell Woods

Woodlands have always been enchanted faerie places, and walking quietly among the trees and wild flowers will bring you closer to these magical beings. You can create your own woodland garden especially to attract faeries into your life, and there are even ways of encouraging them to take up residence in your home.

The Greeks believed that the lives of woodland faeries depended on the health and wellbeing of the trees they inhabited. The best way to gain inspiration is to go for a walk in the woods in springtime to see trees and plants emerge from their winter's rest. Remember that you are likely to be surrounded by nature faeries watching your progress through the wood, so be respectful of all that you encounter there. Never pick or tread on wild flowers—it is not only destructive to the environment but will infuriate faeries. Keep in mind, too, that faeries are said to sleep in old birds' nests and may not take kindly to being disturbed.

"Such a soft floating witchery of sound,
As twilight elfins make, when they at eve
Voyage on gentle gales from faerie land."

Samuel Taylor Coleridge

Finding Nature Faeries

Faeries linked with nature will bring you a revitalizing energy. They have a healing vigor with which they imbue the atmosphere. As you wander through woodland, breathe in this energy for a sense of renewal, tranquility, and inspiration. If you want to be there when faeries are most active, choose a changeover time such as dawn or twilight. You may even be able to hear faerie voices carried in the breeze.

Toadstools

These brightly colored fungi seem to spring up so quickly and unexpectedly that people have always believed them to be linked with the supernatural powers of the world of Faerie. Toadstools are also frequently luminous and poisonous. The red, spotted toadstool Fly Agaric (Amanita muscaria) is the one most often attributed to the world of Faerie; but links with faerie magic are reflected in the names of many others, including Dune Pixie-Hood, Dryad's Saddle, Slender Elf Cap, and Yellow Faerie Club. The Faerie Ring mushroom, growing around a circular plot, marks the boundaries of faerie dancing places.

A faerie sitting among toadstools

Popular Faerie Trees

Certain trees have particular associations with faeries. Their twigs, if twisted together, work an even stronger super-natural power. All of the faeries' favorite trees have guardians who protect them. Never damage a faerie tree, but gifts, such as ribbons tied to the branches, will be well received.

Blackthorn
One of the most sacred trees of Faerie, the blackthorn's fruits—sloes—appear in fall and are jealously guarded by faeries. If you get one of the thorns in your eye, you might well go blind, and if it enters your body, the wound is liable to become infected. In this way, faeries hope to discourage mortals who otherwise show a tendency to steal the sloes and make them into a delicious sloe gin. Blackthorn wood is used for creating divining rods and magic wands that protect their owners from evil.

Elm
In Europe, elms are often linked with elves, and the folk name for the trees is "elven." Elves were believed to live in burial mounds, so the wood selected for coffins was often elm. Meditating near an elm tree enhances communication with nature faeries and devas (see page 36). If you prick an elm leaf with a pin before placing it under your pillow at night, you will dream of your future.

Elder
Supposedly never struck by lightning, the elder tree is thought to have magical powers to open a gateway between the mortal and Faerie worlds. In Danish faerie lore, people who stand under an elder tree on Midsummer's Eve have seen the Faerie King ride by on his white horse, attended by his retinue. Through the world, the elder has mainly beneficial rather than sinister connotations. In Russia, for example, it is believed that elder trees drive away evil faeries and spirits. The Serbs include a twig of elder in wedding ceremonies to bring good luck. In England, however, to put a baby in an elderwood cradle is to have it spirited away, or maliciously pinched and prodded by malevolent faeries.

Hawthorn
A sacred and healing plant, the hawthorn is the tree of the Faerie Queen. "Pixie pears" is another name for hawthorn berries. Faeries are known to meet under hawthorn trees, and it was a springtime custom among mortals to plait crowns of hawthorn blossoms and leave them for the faeries and angels that visit at night. If faeries chose to dance on the crowns, blessings were showered on those who made them. Hawthorn was also used to decorate May poles. Another custom was to attach sprigs of

hawthorn to the cradles of newborn babies to protect them from sickness and from evil faeries or phantoms. Otherwise, it is unlucky to bring hawthorn indoors. Carrying hawthorn gives psychic protection, lifts the spirits and banishes melancholy.

Most witches' gardens included at least one hawthorn hedge, and hawthorn was sometimes known as the "witches' tree." Hawthorn protects a home from lightning and storm damage. Planted with oak and ash, it brings enchantment to a place, allowing mortals to see faeries.

Hazel

Considered to be a faerie tree in Celtic lands, hazel is believed to allow entry into the realm of Faerie. Its wood was sacred, and a taboo fuel for any hearth. Witches' wands were made of hazel and used as divining wands to find underground water.

Oak

Many faeries are thought to live in oak trees. Planting an acorn by the light of the Moon will ensure that faeries bring you good fortune, usually in the form of money. Carrying a piece of oak draws good luck to you.

Rowan

This tree provides powerful protection against wicked faeries. Any mortals traveling on Midsummer's Eve or Hallowe'en were advised

The Blackthorn Faerie, *Cicely Mary Barker, from* Flower Faeries of the Trees

to wear a rowan sprig, and to tuck a sprig into horses' bridles, to guard against being spirited away to Faerie.

Willow

Willow is also supposed to make ideal wands for moonlight magic. The trees are said to uproot themselves at night to follow mortals.

Faerie Flowers

Particular flowering plants are linked with the realm of Faerie. Many are wild flowers but even a few cultivated varieties are associated with faerie magic.

Bluebells

A bluebell wood at dawn, noon, twilight, and midnight is a place of faerie enchantment, so only the bravest should venture into one at these times. It was not only the Irish who believed that to hear a bluebell ring was to hear one's own death knell. Another name for bluebells in Scotland, for example, is "deadmen's bells." The blue flowers also ring at midnight to summon faeries for revelry or festivals. On no account should you pick these enchanted flowers—to do so is to invite misfortune into your life.

Cowslips

Also called "faerie cups," cowslips have bell-shaped flowers in which faeries like to rest. In Shakespeare's "The Tempest," Ariel is often found lying in a cowslip's bell. Faeries have a special fondness for cowslips and are very protective of them. Another name for the plant in the west of England is "culver's keys," because cowslips are thought to unlock the way to hidden faerie treasure. The presence of cowslips is therefore thought to reveal a store of gold nearby.

Dandelions

If you happen to tread upon a dandelion, another plant will soon spring up in its place, because, some believe, dandelions are inhabited by faeries. Dandelion clocks are said to transport faeries and, if you blow on them, you may be granted a wish in return for sending the faeries on their way.

Ferns

Pixies and other faeries shelter beneath ferns and will object to anyone treading on them. According to faerie lore, ferns will also send your secrets in all directions on the four winds, so mortals should not say anything indiscreet near them. In Russia, in midsummer when ferns are yellow, casting a handful of seeds into the air and watching where they fall will reveal hidden gold.

Four-leaved Clover

Although rare, a four-leaved clover may be found occasionally—its reputation for being lucky comes from its ability to break any kind of faerie spell.

Foxgloves

The name "foxglove" comes from the shape of the plant's flowers, which resemble the fingers of a glove. Tiny air-element faeries take refuge from cold winds and rain in its drooping blossoms on chilly evenings. It used to be called "folksglove"—the glove of the "good folk," or faeries, who haunted the banks and

Pansies

A powerful plant, the pansy is used by those who know faerie secrets to make love potions. Faerie lore warns that mortals must never pick a pansy with dew on it because this will cause the death of a loved one. To pick a pansy on a fine day is to invite a storm.

Poppies

To bring faeries into your dreams, take a nap in a field of poppies.

Primroses

Today, we are told never to pick primroses since this woodland plant has become much rarer than it once was. In times gone by, however, posies of primroses were used to convey messages to faeries. Touching a hollow hill or rock with a posy of primroses made the invisible gateway between the mortal world and that of Faerie swing open. Likewise, a bunch of five freshly gathered primroses, especially ones growing near water, was said to open the way to Faerie if placed on a magical standing stone. Primroses were used to safeguard mortals from faerie caprice, too. Posies of primroses were left in cowsheds to deter faeries from stealing milk, and on May Day morning, primrose petals were sprinkled on doorsteps to encourage benevolent faeries to bless the house and all living in it. This custom survived till recently among elderly women in County Roscommon in Ireland.

A naughty faerie places foxgloves on the fox's feet to soften his tread when he prowls around

woody hollows where foxgloves grow. In Norway, it's called "revbielde," meaning foxbell, and it is said in northern Europe that wicked faeries gave these blossoms to the fox that he might put them on his toes to soften his tread when he prowled among the roosts. Foxgloves are sometimes also known as "faerie's gloves" or "faerie bells."

Heather

Having heather in your garden attracts faeries on Midsummer's Eve. Heather is also thought to open the gateway between the mortal world and that of Faerie.

Ragwort

Air-element faeries sometimes use the stems of ragwort as broomsticks on which to fly. "Horse and hattock" are said to be the words used to cast a flying spell on the plant stem.

Rose

Faeries are attracted by the sweet smell and soft petals of roses, which, according to faerie lore, often form an ingredient in love potions. For faerie help in attracting the person you want, sprinkle rose petals on the ground and dance on them, while asking the faeries softly to grant you this wish with their magic.

St John's Wort

The yellow flowers of this plant symbolize the Sun and are thought to dispel wicked faeries.

The Latin name Hypericum from the Greek "huper eikon," meaning "over an apparition," refers to the herb's power to protect mortals from evil supernatural forces. St John's Wort is said to be so obnoxious to wicked faeries that a slight fragrance from it is enough to repel them far away. Sprigs were hung on house and church doors before Midsummer's Eve to protect buildings from wicked faeries, witches, thunder, lightning, and fire. According to faerie lore, if a mortal stepped on St John's Wort, a faerie horse would rise up to take the culprit on a wild ride lasting all night.

Wild Thyme

Wearing a sprig of thyme will increase your ability to see faeries, and you can invite benevolent faeries into your home by planting wild thyme by doors and windows. It can also be used to make a potion that enables mortals to see faeries. For this potion to be effective, the tops of wild thyme and grass must be gathered from the side of a hollow hill.

Faerie Bruises: The mottlings on the blossoms of the foxglove and the cowslip—as well as the spots on butterflies' wings—are said to mark where air-element faeries have placed their fingers

Creating a Faerie Garden

A garden planted with faeries' favorite flowering plants can become a magical place to be. Even if you don't have a garden, make the most of window boxes and pots of plants to encourage faeries to visit.

If you do have a garden, a woodland theme will be most favored by the gentle nature faeries. Keep in mind that faerie enchantment is at its most powerful at times of changeover. Planting on the Spring Equinox (the changeover day from winter to spring), for example, will enhance your garden's magical properties. The practical benefits are that the days will get longer and warmer from this time on, yet deciduous trees will not yet have leaves, so that plants will not be in too much shade. If you plant in fall or early spring, the garden will be at its most enchanting in late spring and early summer.

A Suitable Spot

It's important to choose the right place for your woodland faerie garden. Ideally, this will be in part shade—definitely not in full sun—where the plants will get the benefit of rain and yet the ground will not be constantly waterlogged. Add some old twigs that will rot gradually. This encourages insects that attract birds, and creates the right conditions for faerie fungi, such as toadstools and mushrooms, to grow.

If you have trees in your garden, plant woodland flowers underneath them. Trees that create good conditions for these species include crab apple and wild cherry as well as all those mentioned above.

What To Do

Make sure the hole you dig for each plant is the right size, and leave space around it to allow for growth. Put taller plants at the back where they won't hide the smaller ones. As soon as you have finished planting, water your woodland garden well to give the plants a good start in their new home. Keep the soil damp, but not wet, at all times. If you have planted a miniature woodland garden in a container or pot, you will need to take extra care to ensure the soil is always sufficiently moist.

As well as woodland flowers and plants, include fruit bushes in your garden, if there is space, but never strip these bare, picking all the fruit for yourself, because this makes faeries cross.

To enhance your faerie theme, add decorations in the garden, such as glittery wands, pretty pebbles, shells, and pieces from broken jewelry that glitter with rainbow colors in dappled sunlight.

Build a Faerie Home

Make a cozy place in your garden where faeries can relax, and shelter from wind and rain. Use sticks or twigs, and reinforce the construction's twiggy roof with something waterproof. Line it with comfortable natural material, such as moss, and don't forget to leave an entrance. A terra-cotta saucer filled with rainwater is a lovely place for faeries to bathe, and you could edge your faerie bath with shells to make it really special.

Inviting Faeries Inside

Faeries are fond of being flattered and attended to, and nurturing their goodwill is much better than becoming an object of their ill will, which is most inadvisable. Mortals who show thoughtfulness and respect toward them may be handsomely rewarded with unexpected good fortune, or a stroke of luck when most needed. At the very least, if you welcome a faerie into your home, you will ensure that the atmosphere is harmonious.

Some faeries have an inclination to join mortal households, but whether they are loyal and helpful or discontented and troublesome often depends on how they feel they are being treated—and, since faeries are contrary by nature, this is tricky to predict. However, some simple ways of welcoming faeries into the home have been carried out successfully through the centuries.

Faerie Garden Plants

Faeries love all these woodland flowers and plants.

Anemone blanda	small with delicate green leaves and pretty white flowers in late spring
Bluebell	small with purplish blue bell-like flowers on stalks in late spring
Common violet	small and spreading with purple flowers in early spring
Ferns	common polypody, lamb's tongue, and ladder fern are best, all medium height
Foxglove	tall with long pinkish purple bell-like flowers in late spring or early summer
Greater celandine	small with yellow flowers in early spring
Hedge woundwort	tall with small dark red or purple flower spikes
Herb Robert	medium height with plenty of small dark pink flowers and pretty leaves in late spring
Lily of the valley	small with sweet-smelling small white flowers in early spring
Lords and ladies (Arum)	small plant with cream flowers followed by bright orange berries
Primrose	small with scented pale yellow flowers in early spring
Red campion	medium height with small dark pink flowers in late spring
Red deadnettle	small with red flowers from late spring onward
Lesser periwinkle	small (4in/10cm) and spreading, with dramatic mauve flowers in early spring
Snowdrops	small with bell-shaped white flowers; plant in fall for the first flowers of the year
Solomon's seal	medium with arching stems of small white flowers and very elegant leaves
Sweet woodruff	small with tiny sweet-smelling white flowers
White deadnettle	small with white flowers from late spring onwards
Wild daffodil	small with yellow trumpet-shaped flowers in early spring
Wild strawberry	small with tiny white flowers in early summer followed by tiny strawberries
Wood cranesbill	medium with purple flowers in late spring to early summer
Yellow archangel	small with yellow flowers from late spring onward

Faerie Courtesy

To encourage good faeries to come into your home, and appease the wickeder ones, here are some things you can do.

☆ Leave out small pieces of butter and a little milk as faeries are particularly partial to these.

☆ They also like to bathe somewhere warm, so a shallow bowl of water placed in a suitable spot in your home is welcome.

☆ Grow scented climbing plants, such as honeysuckle, around your window, or keep flowering plants in pots on the sill, then open your window at dawn and twilight to invite in faeries.

☆ Try not to use household or garden products full of chemicals and pesticides, because faeries tend to find these repellent.

Attracting a Brownie

It may be that you would like a brownie (see page 78) to join your household. If so, keep in mind that this faerie enjoys a well-kept house with cheerful mortals who maintain a reliable and predictable routine. Like other faeries, the brownie delights in small gifts of milk and butter. He will move in only if he decides that you are the type of human worthy of his loyalty. If you continue to make your home warm and inviting to the brownie, and you both do nice things for one another, a trusting relationship will grow. You will find that the brownie is a powerful boost to the positive

A faerie hiding among nettles

Good advice

A century or so ago in Ireland, Lady Francesca Wilde advised: "Never drain your wine-glass at a feast, nor the poteen flask, nor the milk-pail; and never rake out all the fire at night, it looks mean, and the faeries like a little of everything going, and to have the hearth comfortable and warm when they come in to hold a council after all the mortal people have gone to bed."

energy in your home, so that all living there, pets included, enjoy good luck and a healthy mind and body.

Protection from malevolent faeries

If you are at all concerned that you or your home may be receiving the attention of troublesome faeries, it is worth putting some safeguards in place. Here are some ways to repel those faeries you would prefer not to have around:

☆ Sprinkle a little bit of salt on all of your windowsills.

☆ Iron, particularly in the form of an iron horseshoe on your front door, is generally effective.

☆ On the door of any room that you suspect the faeries of entering—the kitchen or the bedroom are the most likely trouble spots—hang a pincushion stuck with pins.

☆ A copy of the Bible, or a crucifix, wards off bad faeries. Make the sign of a cross on anything you would prefer the faeries to leave alone. For example, to prevent faeries from nibbling and jumping around on a freshly baked cake, make the sign of a cross on it.

☆ Faeries find noise made by mortals annoying, and they particularly dislike the sound of church bells. Ringing bells in your home regularly can be enough to discourage troublesome faeries from wanting to set up residence there.

☆ Always place shoes with toes pointing away from the bed to repel visits from mischievous faeries who arrive at night to matt and twist your hair.

☆ If you are walking at night in a rural district, turn one of your garments, such as a glove, inside out to ward off malevolent faeries.

How to See Faeries

Most faerie sightings take place as the light—either sunlight or moonlight—is transforming at a particular time of day or night. You are most likely to see a faerie at May Eve, Midsummer's Eve, or Hallowe'en which to the Celts marked the changeover from the old year to the new.

Changeover periods enhance the ability to see faeries, which is why young teenaged girls, such as the two at Cottingley, have always been especially likely to see them.

Faeries, being private and secretive, do not wish to be observed by mortals, so a steady gaze is needed to notice them before they disappear in the blink of an eye. If you ever find a four-leaved clover, carry it with you to allow you to see even the faeries who aim to remain invisible.

Stones, Salves, and Elderberries

Mortals have reported being able to see faeries if they look through a self-bored stone—a stone in which a natural hole has been made by flowing water. Otherwise, a special salve applied to the eyelids has the same effect. Some mortals used to know the secret recipe for this salve, including the faerie doctors who had spent time in the world of Faerie. The salve is rumored to include four-leaved clovers ground to a powder.

Elderberry wine is considered to be faerie nectar and drinking it is said to enable mortals to see faeries. To draw faeries near to you, add dried elderberries to an incense mixture.

"I Believe in Faeries"

To be given the chance to see faeries, you must believe in them. In "Peter Pan," J.M. Barrie takes this idea further—as Tinkerbell is dying, Peter Pan calls out to dreaming children:

> *"Do you believe in faeries? . . . If you believe in faeries, clap your hands!"*

(Peter Pan, Act IV)

The Faerie Feller's Master Stroke,
Richard Dadd, 1855–64, oil on canvas

Tinkerbell comes back to life, sustained by children's acceptance of her existence.

As children, our minds are open to new and different experiences. Sadly, adults' minds tend to become more closed and cynical. A "childlike" belief is not always well considered in our society. However, our inner worlds are richer places, if we look around us with curiosity and a willingness to believe in things outside our complete understanding.

Drawing Energy to Your Third Eye

Faeries occupy a realm between the physical and spiritual worlds so, to see them, you need to develop your psychic awareness. In your body, your capacity for psychic awareness is situated in your "third eye," which lies in the center of your forehead.

☆ Sit cross-legged on the floor in a calm space where you will not be disturbed. Close your eyes and breathe slowly in and out. Make your out breath last as long as your in breath. Notice how your body feels and where there is any tension. Focus on breathing into that area until you feel it relax. Allow the muscles around your eyes to relax, then feel tension ease away from the point between your eyes outward. Let your jaw relax, allowing your mouth to drop open slightly. Once all your muscles are relaxed, become aware that you are breathing in energy.

The Sight

The ability to see faeries is simply called "the sight." It may be granted to the seventh son of a seventh son, or the seventh daughter of a seventh daughter, particularly if he or she has red hair.

☆ Visualize yourself surrounded by healing, energizing light. It helps to imagine this energizing light as a color—I think of glowing pink or orange, which to me have soothing but also uplifting associations. Now stretch your arms outward slowly, and circle them upward. Visualize that you are encircling light and energy in the form of your chosen color. When your hands meet above your head, join them in the prayer position and draw the life-giving energy to your third eye in the middle of your forehead. Feel yourself to be "at one" with the vibrant energy of the universe, revitalized and serene.

Nature Meditation

To connect with faeries, you need a willingness to open your mind and heart. "You have to be content to know that you love that tree, and you want to love it more," said Ella Young, a poet and storyteller who communed with faeries in western Ireland, "and you know it's alive and you want to come closer to it."

First, find a quiet place to sit outside. A woodland area is ideal. You must be alone and sure of being undisturbed.

☆ Inhale and imagine a wave of green light rising from the earth beneath you, rising up your body to connect you with the earth below. Exhale and sense a wave of golden light flowing down from the heavens through your body, connecting you with the sun and stars. Do this several times until you feel relaxed and charged with the energy of earth and sky.

☆ Notice the trees and plants around you. Visualize light extending from your heart to connect with each one. Enjoy this feeling of oneness and inner peace.

☆ Ask for a message from the Faerie realm. You may feel a light, joyful energy, or particular words or images may come suddenly to mind.

☆ Always remember to thank the faeries before you leave.

A girl meditating with a faerie guide

Index

Dedicated to my mother, Lady Warren of County Cork, Ireland

I would like to thank Liz Dean, Marion Paull, and Carmel Edmonds for the editorial expertise they have brought to the creation of this book.

Picture credits

The Bridgeman Art Library
Pages 6, 9, 17, 21, 31, 60, 65, 69, 85, 89, 96, 101, 103, 105, 118, 121, 135, 137, and 140

Mary Evans
Pages 3, 13, 15, 23, 33, 46, 49, 72, 91, 95, 114, and 127

Topfoto
Pages 37, 41, 125, 129, 131, 133, and 155

The Art Archive
Page 77

Frederick Warne & Co.
Page 145, image reproduced by kind permission of Frederick Warne & Co., copyright © The Estate of Cicely Mary Barker, 1940, 1990

Glenn Hill/NMeM/Science & Society Picture Library
Pages 138 and 139